HOW TO BOUNCE BACK QUICKLY AFTER LOSING YOUR JOB

Holly S. Smith

VGM Career Horizons
a division of *NTC Publishing Group*
Lincolnwood, Illinois USA

Library of Congress Cataloging-in-Publication Data

Smith, Holly S.
    How to bounce back quickly after losing your job / by Holly S.
Smith.
        p.   cm. -- (VGM opportunities series)
    ISBN 0-8442-4167-9
    1. Unemployment--Psychological aspects. 2. Unemployment.
3. Employees, Dismissal of. I. Title. II. Series.
HD5708.S63   1993
650.14--dc20   92-34630
                                                       CIP

Contents

About the Author

Holly S. Smith is a freelance journalist who enjoys writing just about anything, but most frequently covers the areas of business and marketing, education, the environment, music and the arts, travel, and wildlife. Previously, she worked as an advertising copywriter and served as publisher of *Advance* magazine. Her articles and special sections have appeared in publications that include *The Cincinnati Enquirer, The Cincinnati Post, The Kentucky Post, Travel Talk, AAA World,* and various industry publications. She is also a contributing writer and editor for *CREW News,* a publication of the Center for the Reproduction of Endangered Wildlife at The Cincinnati Zoo and Botanical Gardens.

For her work, she has received awards from the International Association of Business Communicators, the International Newspaper Association of Marketing Executives, the Ohio Newspaper Advertising Executives, the American Advertising Federation, the Advertising Club of Cincinnati, and the Cincinnati Business/Professional Advertising Association.

Her most recent project involved traveling to some of the world's most endangered wildlife reserves and talking with both local residents and park officials on their hopes and fears about the future of these habitats. She also is writing and illustrating a series of children's books and has penned three fiction novels.

Foreword
A Special Word to Friends and Family

If you have previously lost a job to layoffs or termination, you realize just how awful it feels: the anger, the hurt, the feeling of betrayal; not to mention the embarrassment of having it happen, the shame of telling others, and the guilt of thinking over and over again that there is something that could have been said or done to prevent it. It's almost too much for a heart and mind to bear.

You—family and friends—are the ones the unemployed are counting on, whether they are aware of it yet or not. They need your love, encouragement, and support, and they need you to show it every day. They need you to understand how badly they feel, and to confirm that they are indeed winners, that they have valuable talents and skills they will soon be using again.

To stay motivated, they need to feel your confidence and hear your words of love and strength until they grasp your belief in them. It will help them eventually to believe in themselves and to get back on their feet and get going again more quickly.

It's a double-edged sword, however, for this is also an experience that the unemployed workers must face by themselves, and each person reacts differently to the pressure and emotions involved. You may even be the target of their anger and disappointment; expect short tempers and tears and quiet, brooding spells for a while. And, even if they brush you off, keep encouraging them—they need it. Deep inside they're absorbing all that caring until they are full enough with strength and courage and hope to set out on their own.

I never quite understood such anger and pain could exist until it happened to me, and without a wonderful circle of family and friends to give me love and encouragement, you might not be reading this book right now. But I hope you take these words to heart, and pass them on to the ones for whom you care, because job loss is painful; to me, the deepest pain next to death, for I had thrown my life into my work and a career that I loved, and when I lost it, I thought I had nothing.

As, most likely, does anyone else in the same situation.

But with encouragement and love, the confidence eventually surfaces, as hesitantly as does the belief that we can succeed again. And, we can change our lives, often into something we would never have thought of had the job loss not occurred, and almost always into something far better than we had before.

So, please tell them, and show them, how much you believe in them, for that sharing of the heart and understanding of feelings is one of the greatest gifts we can give to one another.

Acknowledgments

To Cliff, Jerry, Jo, and Ronnie
for getting me into it,

to Alan
for getting me out of it,

and to Trevor,
without whom it never would have happened.

Also, a special thanks to each and every person with whom I spoke: the counselors and managers who gave their valuable advice and expertise, the families who gave their encouragement, and especially the hundreds of workers who shared their emotions and experiences to help others through the pain and discouragement and to motivate them to make the job loss a positive turning point in their lives.

Introduction

Right now, you probably feel like hell.

Let's face it, if you've picked up this book, you've either just lost your job or you think the ax might fall soon. Your stomach is in knots. You're probably dizzy, anxious, and bleary-eyed from lack of sleep. You've been forgetting simple things, and you're constantly snapping at your family and friends. Getting up in the morning is more difficult than ever.

The stress of not knowing what's coming next in your life is a feeling that crosses all demographic boundaries of those on the firing line. Whether you're female or male; twenty or fifty; an assistant, manager, or company president who's pulling in $15,000 or $100,000 a year; the symptoms are all the same.

But the good news is, those who have been through it *do* recover. And then, they move on and *succeed.*

This book will give the facts to you straight, from ways to watch for warning signs and how to handle the final meeting or interview, through your first day off the job and beyond. We'll cover your feelings and questions and plans of action and rights, as well as ways to find inexpensive emotional and legal counseling, if you need it. We'll also talk about the process from your employer's point of view, so you can see how the job loss situation is set up and how you can fight back effectively.

But the bottom line is to remember who *you* are. Your skills, your talents, your goals and dreams are what really matter, because they are what will make you happy in life. Don't let your company, through the trauma of termination or layoff, take them away from you; instead, think of this as a learning experience, an exciting turning point that is giving you the opportunity to explore your dreams.

In life, it is the strongest people who are presented with the greatest challenges, so keep believing in yourself—no matter how desperate the situation seems.

And step forward with the knowledge that you *will* succeed again.

Due to limited space, some of the examples used in this book have been compiled from several different interviews. To protect the anonymity of each source, all names and companies are fictional, unless otherwise indicated.

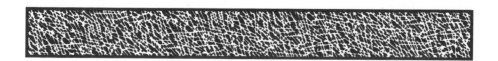

1

Warning Signs:
Paranoia or
Precognition?

Over eight million people.

That's approximately how many workers the U.S. Department of Labor reports as being currently unemployed in our country. To give you a rough idea of the magnitude of that number, picture the cities of Los Angeles and Chicago combined . . . or nearly the entire population of Sweden . . . or every seat in an average football stadium filled during every Superbowl game—for the next one hundred years!

And, of this very real part of our population, more than half are "job losers," the rather depressing term used to describe workers who lost their jobs due to layoffs or termination. No prerequisites are necessary to become a part of this group; regardless of age, gender, heritage, or status, each person who joins takes on the challenge of picking up his or her past and starting over again, often in a completely new life.

Yet, out of so many workers who were dismissed from their jobs, few took time to notice the obvious exit signs—and even fewer took protective action. Why did they hesitate? Wouldn't it have been more logical to face the situation head-on by asking for details on their employment status at the first hint of suspicion that their jobs were on the line?

As you know, it's not that simple. You may feel frozen and scared; you would rather not know the inevitable. It's easier to avoid the situation than to stand up and do something about it. Perhaps you're angry, you hate your boss, and you think you just won't care if you lose your job—who needs the company hassles, anyway? Or, maybe you think that you're just being paranoid about the subtle changes going on around you; they probably don't mean anything at all. Or do they?

No matter how you feel, if you suspect your job is on the line, the most important thing you can do right now is to prepare for a possible layoff. Other employees targeted for termination or layoff might work on in blissful ignorance or fear until the very last day, when they'll wander off into oblivion without benefits or references and only a bleak job future on the horizon. But you're not like them, and picking up this book was just the first step to prove it. From now on you're going to take control of your life and your future.

The difference is that you're not a victim, you're a fighter who is strong, smart, and willing to stand up for your rights and get the benefits you deserve from an employer to whom you have devoted years, even decades, of your talent and energy. Want more incentive to fight back? Just think about all the times you missed with your family and friends because your job had to come first. How about the efforts you have made to expand your function and responsibility within the company, or how your department has improved in efficiency and attitude since you came on board? And what about all the times you took work home or on vacation with you, either in content or in mind?

Like many people, your job is the center of your life, a place where you are able to use your skills and intelligence on a daily basis and bring home a paycheck that proves your worth. Including commuting to and from work, lunches, company functions, business trips, and time spent thinking about your job when you're not there, you probably are in the "employee" mindset for 60 to 80 hours each week—that adds up to a minimum of 3,000 hours each year, or nearly 130,000 hours over the course of the average worker's career. Still, multiply that 3,000 hours (or more!) by the number of years you have been with your company and you'll find you have a lot of time invested. And that's *your* time, *your* life that has been dedicated to that job every day; so don't walk away empty-handed.

But first, let's take a look at the top unemployment warning signs, just to make sure you're not worrying without reason. Pick up a pen and check off all the signals that sound familiar and fill in a few sample situations to document when you noticed a particular occurrence (see chart 1.1). Then, examine the Job Saver responses in chart 1.2 to find out questions you can ask when you notice these warning signs, and whether the responses of your supervisors and co-workers indicate that you're still on a safe job track (see case 1).

Some of the best warning signals, however, will come from your own body, which will often react to stressful circumstances your mind refuses to accept (see case 2). Let's see how you have been feeling lately; check all the applicable symptoms on chart 1.3 and write down the approximate date you noticed each one.

By now, you're beginning to be convinced that it's not all in your head and there's more to your anxiety than daily stress. You don't need a

CHART 1.1

Some Common Pink-Slip Predictors

- The economy and your field are down in profits and job openings.

- Your company hasn't hired anyone for some time, and several workers, or several hundred workers, have been laid off recently.

- Everyone knows your company is in financial trouble, or rumors of a corporate merger or buyout are circulating throughout your office, or the community, or even the media.

- You find your assignments redistributed to coworkers, and you are given no new projects.

- Your supervisor starts to encourage you to look for broader horizons; the company isn't your only option for the future.

- Your supervisor questions your progress much more than usual.

- You notice your supervisor writing down things after he or she talks with you about progress or performance.

- You are called into your supervisor's office more often than usual to discuss your work or your attitude.

- You are called to the personnel office or your supervisor's office to answer questions about a particular project or incident, although you may not be informed of any problems. Everyone eludes your questions.

- Your coworkers have an attitude change; when you're around, they stop talking, avert their eyes, or smile sympathetically.

- You have more than one fair or poor rating on your performance review.

- You can't get the hang of your job and your boss agrees with you.

- You have received multiple complaints about your performance from clients, coworkers, or the company.

- You're passed over for a promotion or a raise more than once.

- You dislike your job, and everyone knows it.

- Computer passwords, locks, or security codes are suddenly changed, and you don't receive the new ones.

CHART 1.2

Job-Savers: Questions and Responses

Questions you should ask	Answers you might receive	Job on the line?
1. How am I doing on the job in general?	You did very well in your last performance review.	Probably not
	I wouldn't worry about it.	Maybe
	We've had to warn you more than once to improve	Definitely
2. Is there anything I can do to improve my performance?	You're doing an excellent job, as far as I know.	Probably not
	Well, as we discussed previously . . .	Maybe
	Don't bother doing anything.	Definitely
3. Why am I not getting any new assignments?	We're preparing you for a new project/position.	Probably not
	We think Joe Smith can do a better job, but don't worry, you'll get more.	Maybe
	I don't know/can't talk about it.	Definitely
4. Have I done anything to upset you or upper management?	No, I'm just feeling well/tired/under stress.	Probably not
	Well, there was that one incident, but we'll talk about it later.	Maybe
	I wouldn't worry about it.	Maybe
5. Is there anything to the rumors I've been hearing about our company's financial situation/merge/ buyout/downsizing?	What rumors?	Probably not
	I don't know anything about it.	Maybe
	I've also heard rumors, but nothing is certain.	Definitely
	I can't talk about it.	Definitely

CHART 1.3

Body Stress Symptoms

Physical

1. Headache

2. Stomachache

3. Muscle twitches

4. Shaky hands/jitters

5. Blurred vision

6. Insomnia

7. Cold symptoms/sore throat

8. Diarrhea

9. Low energy level

Mental

1. Forgetfulness

2. General apathy for work

3. Paranoia/feeling watched

4. Constant anger or guilt

5. Mental fatigue/inability to solve problems/reduced creativity and determination

6. Negative job attitude

7. Depression/crying

8. Fear/avoidance of superiors and co-workers

9. Short temper

vacation—you need to take action immediately and find out what's really going on.

But how? You don't want to pry, spy, or lie to gain information about the status of your future with your employer. Well, you don't have to. The information is right under your nose if you know where to look. If you're fairly certain that you might soon become an unemployment statistic, here are a few steps that will help you find out the truth of the matter and strengthen your on-the-job image at the same time.

STEP ONE: START ASKING QUESTIONS

You may be shy or scared, but what do you have to lose? Only sleep and your mind if you don't find out who is saying what about your position. Usually this process is a lonely effort, but if you have a true friend you can trust within the company, talk about your feelings with that person and ask him or her to help you watch for warning signs.

Be wary, however, of actions that might place your friend's job in jeopardy; for example, don't encourage someone in the personnel department to swipe your file. Just ask him or her to keep both eyes and ears open. If your friendship is strong, you'll be informed of any warning signs as soon as they occur, and your suspicions will be confirmed—or denied—with empathy.

STEP TWO: DOCUMENT EVERYTHING

If you think you're headed for a layoff situation, consistent proof of your good work could help you keep your job. And, if your company has marked you for termination, evidence of poor performance, misuse of time, or rule-bending is a great way to save your supervisors from paying unemployment benefits or giving you the full severance package. Evidence to refute any charges will go a long way to help your case. In termination cases, especially, you can bet your employer is writing down everything you do, from phone calls and performance reviews to the exact time you walk in and out of the office each day as well as any offhand remarks you make about the company. Watch your back—and your mouth.

Also, when you start to suspect job loss might be in your near future, keep a detailed diary (see chart 1.4) of everything you do, when you do it, and why you did it. Layoffs and terminations are serious business, regardless of the type of industry or company in which you work, so don't underestimate the actions your employer can take against you. If

Keeping a Detailed Work Diary

Date	Time	Action
7/25	8:00	I arrived at work.
	8:15	Talked with supervisor about progress on Jones project. Supervisor said I need to work more quickly and pay attention to detail. I brought up the fact that I am three days ahead of schedule, and I caught an error in a budget calculation by the company that would have cost us $4,000. Supervisor agreed that my progress was improving.
	8:20	Continued work on Jones project with coworkers.
	9:00	Department director needed quick report. I volunteered.
	9:10	Jenkins called. I told her our progress on the project for her company and asked her if she had any changes or suggestions. She requested we shorten our deadline by two days, so I transferred her to my supervisor to verify that this would be possible.
	9:25	Finished director's report and submitted it for typing.
	9:45	Met with Anderson about retail project after doing a bit more work on the Jones project. We agreed we need more color and creativity in the layout, so we decided to ask the art department for new ideas. Talked with department head about concerns and needs. We were promised three new ideas by 3 p.m.
	10:00	Supervisor requested update on Murphy file. Sat down in office and showed my progress and the work that is still left to do.
	10:15	Went to typist for director's report—still not finished. Requested it in the next 15 minutes and mentioned the importance of the report and who needed it.
	10.20	Director came in and requested report. I explained I had finished it before 9:30 and that the typists were working on it. I told him I had just checked on the status and it would be finished in the next ten minutes. Started working on Murphy project ideas.
	10:25	Took call for accounting department. Said I'd be happy to transfer the caller.
	10:28	Checked on director's report. Still not typed!
	10:30	Director came in angry, demanding report. I calmed him down and asked him to walk with me to the typist, who immediately started on the job. We watched her finish it, just to be sure. Director said I did a great job; wasn't my fault typing was slow.

you believe you are being unfairly discharged, your documents will back up your arguments against losing your job. Either way, from the moment you start noticing warning signs, take notes on everything that takes place no matter how much time it takes to write down. It's important. (See case #3.)

STEP THREE: COPY YOUR FILES AND REMOVE EVERYTHING THAT IS RIGHTFULLY YOURS

You may feel silly doing it, but if you don't, your files (proof of your good work, personal notes, future ideas, positive comments from customers and your employer, phone numbers and contacts) may all disappear—forever. If you clean out your files after being laid off or terminated, you can bet there will be someone else standing there with you keeping an eye on what you take. Even if you're allowed to clean out your desk alone, you're going to be too numb to think about which materials you should remove. Besides, after you have just been informed that you have lost your job, you won't want to stick around your office longer than necessary, believe me.

One caution, though: Don't make it look as if you're clearing out for good. Just copy the files you feel are important, a few at a time, along with other projects on which you're currently working, or before and after hours, if you're allowed. Unless it's a breach of security, you have the right to keep duplicate records of your work at home, but if anyone asks what you're doing, simply say you're cleaning up to make room for new projects and ideas.

STEP FOUR: WORK YOUR BEST

Whatever you do, don't let your job performance slide now. It's a sure sign to employers that you don't care any more, and a great reason to document for letting you go. Come to work a little early, stay a little late, and keep your lunch, phone calls, and breaks to a minimum. Be on time and be prepared for every meeting. An employer who is making a layoff decision or looking for reasons to terminate someone will be additionally tough on him or her, whether in front of others or on a one-on-one basis. It's their job to highlight the negative notes in your personnel file. Don't let them!

If you don't know an answer to a question your supervisor asks, say,

"Although I don't know right now, I would be happy to look up that sales figure/call Mr. Jones and find out/check with our regional office/ etc." Show your employer that you are a hard worker who is willing to find out anything you don't know. And, don't forget, document everything.

STEP FIVE: SMILE

The most obvious way of showing your stress is by looking and acting worried, bitter, or frightened. Take a deep breath, act confidently, keep your chin up, and smile.

Your employer has your head on the chopping block, so why not bounce the ball back into his or her court? Constantly ask about your performance: "How am I doing on the Jefferson job?" "What did you think of my work on project XYZ?" "I made my sales/quality goal for the month. Don't you agree that my work is improving?" Then keep a record of his or her responses.

If you look vulnerable you'll seem guilty, so stand up straight and keep your head high. Looking confident will help you become confident, boost your image with your coworkers, and give you the courage to go after the benefits you well deserve.

_____ CASE 1 _____
Distant Thunder: Don't Ignore the Changes

"I knew something was wrong when our department supervisor kept calling Mary into her office for long talks behind closed doors," says Diane, a copywriter for a large advertising firm. "I've seen people fired by the company before, and the pattern is always the same. The atmosphere in the department is cold and tense, and every action of that particular employee is scrutinized. There was a definite attitude change in management about Mary's work, too; she is very creative and conscientious, but our supervisor kept cutting her down for every little thing. It was as if, all of a sudden, she couldn't do anything right, even though we all had previously looked up to her."

But Diane says Mary still didn't think she would be fired, even though several employees mentioned her supervisor's change in attitude toward her. "She knew she had an excellent work record, that she had a lot of friends in the company and a very bright future," Diane continues. "But it wasn't poor performance, it was simply that a change in management had led to a personality difference between Mary and our new vice-president. She was too outspoken and ambitious, and he felt she was undermining his job. But Mary thought she was untouchable. We all saw it coming, but she just wasn't prepared. I think she'll land on her feet, but it hit her pretty hard."

—————— CASE 2 ——————
Vital Signs: What Your Mind Isn't Telling You

"Before I lost my job, I felt terrible all the time," remembers Claudia, a former public relations coordinator for a community college. "I knew my manager hated me, which made it horrible to go into work every day. I felt tired and run-down, I didn't have the energy to do anything. I was nervous because I felt she was watching me all the time to see if I would make a mistake. I had headaches and stomachaches, and it was hard to get out of bed."

Claudia says the pressure she had to deal with at work each day didn't make the situation any easier. "I knew my performance was being monitored every minute, and I felt that no matter what I did my manager would criticize me. I was trying to do my best work, but I was so depressed about the whole thing—and so angry. It wasn't fair for her to treat me that way, and she wouldn't allow me to prove that I could do the job; plus, I just felt so sick the whole time. It was almost a relief when I was let go because I didn't have to deal with the situation anymore."

—————— CASE 3 ——————
Big Brother: What You Think Your Employer Doesn't Know

"Whenever we have to terminate someone, we keep track of everything they do, from when they go to the bathroom to what they say on the phone and in meetings," says John, a claims examiner at a major insurance company. "My boss has to document every little detail. For example, before one guy was fired, the record listed things like: '10:00, made personal phone call for six minutes; 11:15, was rude to customer; 2:00, spoke up in meeting, was pushy, and wouldn't work with rest of project team.' Any action, any response, any violation of procedure—no matter how small—is recorded to enforce our case."

John adds that his company notes details such as work progress, whether assignments are on time, if the employee is keeping up with the rest of the staff, whether he or she follows procedures (dress code, chain of command, proper paperwork, etc.), and the opinions of both clients and co-workers about the employee. "Personality clashes, brought on by a change in management or staff members, are often a cause of employee dismissal," he notes. "Just as in any fast-paced field, there's a lot of employee turnover, which means people have to adjust to different management styles in a short period of time. People who aren't flexible enough to change with the system are seen as slow or difficult to work with, and the things they feel they are doing correctly can be the very actions that are used against them."

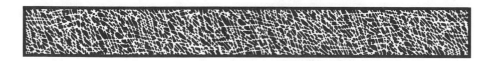

2

Setting the Trap: Layoffs and Termination from the Company's Point of View

Believe it or not, layoffs and terminations are not something your company enjoys. For them it may be a necessary action for a variety of reasons, many of which have nothing to do with you at all (see chart 2.1). An unprofitable year, a slowing industry, and new technology can often lead to the termination of thousands of jobs. Perhaps the company can't afford you, your position has become obsolete, or your department realizes that it can operate with fewer employees—and you were the last one hired.

Changes in management also can create problems. Sometimes a new person in power will find he or she has personality conflicts with the current employees, who are used to the previous manager's style. A new manager also may want to bring his or her own assistant, or he or she may want to hire a "star" whose work is familiar—perhaps even a relative or personal friend. In any case, these changes can put your position in danger, so be prepared to be flexible—and keep your eyes open for subtle alterations or reductions in your responsibilities.

Finally, you may have simply screwed up once too often and it's time to take the consequences. An out-of-control expense account, wasting company time, or abusing privileges are all mistakes that can wind up with or without a second-chance warning. Other situations include bad politics with clients or superiors, a habit of tardiness to or absence from work, substance abuse, or out-and-out crime (stealing company materials, embezzling funds, making extensive long-distance phone calls, threatening other employees). Don't be shocked, it happens—and in these cases you usually won't get another try.

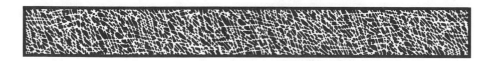

CHART 2.1

Why the Jobs Disappear

Employer-caused loss:
- Local, state, or national downturn in the economy

- A slowing industry

- Company losses and debts force cost-cutting measures

- Company buyouts or management changes

- Changes in technology make jobs obsolete

- An overflow of qualified workers

- Changes in procedure combine several duties in one job

Employee-caused loss:
- Poor work habits

- Personality clashes with management

- Constant tardiness or sick days

- Misuse of company equipment

- Illegal substance abuse

- Sabotage

- Verbal and physical infractions of rules

- Any criminal act

Basically, your company wants to protect its image and assets, including products, property, and future production. Even if your employer has an at-will firing policy, however, to make a case for your dismissal, whether by layoff or termination, they will usually document their reasons in case they need to prove them later.

THE SET-UP

If you suspect you're going to be laid off or fired, you can usually guess the reasons. Even if you aren't sure it's going to happen, you can follow the steps in the first chapter to get a better picture of the situation. Now is your opportunity to fight back and prove your good work and value to the company *before* the axe falls on your head.

When the possibility has been suggested to management, most companies won't make an immediate decision in favor of layoffs or termination. If it comes to cutting back staff, upper management will usually first try to save money elsewhere, by chopping expenditures, downsizing budgets, conserving resources more efficiently, and so on. When the only solution seems to be layoffs, however, larger companies most often inform their middle managers of the number of employees they need to cut back, leaving them to decide who stays and who heads for the door. For some of the factors they look at when making their decision, see chart 2.2, and fill in your own qualifications.

If you think you're going to be fired, however, your company is looking for *proof* of unsatisfactory work, misuse of company time and funds, poor attitude, and so on, and it could take weeks or even months to gather enough information to justify their action. They will document *everything* and possibly even ask you questions about your performance or a suspicious situation over and over again.

At first glance, the manager asking the questions may seem dense; you may think he or she hasn't been listening when your answers are repeated with wrong dates, times, or productivity levels. Take caution: Your company does know your previous answers. You're just being examined for slip-ups. Have your story straight and stick to it, and don't be afraid to ask if there is a problem.

If the person questioning you says there's no problem yet, he or she may be searching for an unintentional admission of guilt. Simply reply, "If you can't tell me whether or not there's a problem, I'm afraid I can't give you any relevant answers." Period.

CHART 2.2

Making the Layoff Decision

If your company is headed for the downsizing trail, which factors affect management's choices for who goes and who stays?

	–5 points	0 points	+5 points
• Length of employment	less than one year	1–10 years	10+ years
• Work record	poor or fair	average	excellent
• Importance of function (Could someone else do your job, or do it better?)	yes	maybe	no
• Seasonal productivity (Does your company profit year-round, or only during the holidays or the summer?)	yes (seasonal)		no (year-round)
• Technology and equipment (Could computers or machines replace you and cost the company less?)	yes	maybe	no
• Your skills (Are you learning new functions and keeping up with job technology?)	no	sometimes	yes
• Prospects for moving within the company (Are you a valuable investment to your employer?)	no	not sure	yes
• Your flexibility (Do you adjust to changes in management and procedures? Are you willing to learn and suggest ideas?)	not usually	sometimes	yes
	Total	Total	Total

Grand Total: _____ points

Point scale:

–40 to –20	–20 to +20	+20 to +40
good layoff candidate	possible layoff candidate	unlikely layoff candidate

CHART 2.3

Guidelines Your Company Must Follow During Layoffs and Terminations

- It is illegal to terminate an employee's position due to:

–race	–national origin
–color	–handicap
–gender	–labor union status
–religion	–veteran's status

- Job contracts:

  A contract is an agreement on the conditions of your job between you and your employer, and this agreement can be either oral or written. If this agreement on the terms of your employment is included in a written document, however, a court will uphold the document as your employer's legally binding obligation to you. Typical agreements are often included in application forms, letters stating the job offer, employee handbooks, and company manuals.

- Types of job loss you should understand:
  –*Firing* means the employee is being dismissed for a cause such as theft, sabotage, trading corporate secrets, and so on.

  –*Layoff* usually indicates that the worker may be called back for employment at a future time.

  –*Termination* suggests that an employee did not fulfill his or her original work expectations, usually due to poor work performance.

  –*Position elimination* occurs most often during the downsizing of a company, or during a corporate merger, and are due to the work environment rather than employee performance.

- Release of legal rights:

  When some companies discharge workers, they offer additional cash or benefits in exchange for the employee signing a release of his or her legal rights. Requirements the employer must follow include:

  –Employees must be aware of the fact that they are releasing their legal rights when they sign.

  –Employees must receive something of value in exchange for their signature, something in addition to the severance and benefits they are normally entitled to.

  –Employees must sign the release voluntarily.

CHART 2.4

Pitfalls That Scare Management During Layoffs and Terminations

- **Discrimination:**
  If you're an employee 55 or older, a woman or member of any other minority, handicapped, or any of the other categories on the list in chart 2.3, your company will be very careful about how they handle your job loss situation. They will not only back up their decision with adequate documentation, but they also will step carefully if someone is hired to take your place, particularly if that person is younger, male, Caucasian, or a combination of characteristics that would put the company in an awkward discriminatory situation.

- **Documentation:**
  Your company wants to be certain they aren't slapped with a wrongful discharge suit, so they will take great measures to back up their decision.

- **Legal Rights:**
  Your company must be sure you know you are signing your legal rights away when you sign the agreement, and they must offer you something of value in return.

- **Implied Promises:**
  Employment contracts, job security, protection during "whistleblower" cases where an employee called in the legal forces on other employees breaking the law, and good faith (or fairness) can all be implied through oral agreements between employer and employee. Your company wants to make sure there have been no implications such as those listed above that could result in a court case after your termination.

- **Security:**
  If your job places you in the "inner circle" of company knowledge, your employer will make sure you do not release your knowledge to anyone outside of the company.

- **Employee Reaction:**
  Timing and environment are crucial to keeping an employee from blowing up or acting out and damaging company property, image, and co-worker relations after he or she is let go.

CHART 2.5

A Few More Job Loss Definitions

Firing at will: When an employer hires an individual to work at the company for an indefinite period of time, this employment is regarded as "employment at will" that may be terminated at any time and for any reason by either the worker or the employer.

Reasons to Seek Legal Counsel

Wrongful discharge: If you are fired in violation of a company policy, such as if you called in authorities on illegal actions by your employer or if you refused to lie. This also covers situations that involve contract claims, either written or in states where verbal contract agreements are binding.

Violation of the Antidiscrimination Laws: If you think you may have been let go due to your race, gender, age, physical disability, national origin, religion, or pregnancy, these laws may apply.

Violation of the Plant Closing Act: If you are not given the number of days' notice before layoff and the amount of money that has been agreed on. This law also covers the closing of industrial plants and office work-force reduction.

Note: Each of these laws may vary from state to state, so check with your lawyer or employment bureau to find out the details that apply to your area. And remember, taking a case to court can often take time (one year or more) and money (thousands of dollars in legal fees), so seek advice, and a second and third opinion, before you decide it is the route you should take.

THE SEARCH

To conduct a thorough investigation of the layoff and termination possibilities, your company will most likely need input from several sources: industry contacts, clients, co-workers, and so on. You can find out more about what is going on by keeping in contact with these people or by talking with others you know in the company or the field, and by being open about the situation. They'll see that you're not afraid to discuss your concerns, and most likely they'll be willing to share their information and advice, unless they have received a direct order of silence or it's a conflict of interest with their own position (see case 7).

YOUR ACTION

Although there's no law stating that it is your given right to be able to do so, most companies will allow you to look at your personnel file at any time, whether alone or under the supervision of a superior. Beat your employer to the punch. Ask if you can see your file. *Today.* Look for any new entries, changes in your performance reviews, or clues leading to the possibility of layoff or termination. You may not be allowed to copy any information, so bring a notebook. If you find something that you don't understand or that makes your record look different than you remember, write it down for your own files.

Then, sit down with your supervisor or a personnel executive and ask about it—how the notation was made, when, why, and by whom. When you know the answers, you can better understand your company's procedures and show your concern for your future there. And, if there's a notation you feel is biased or unfair, you can also defend your position with a written rebuttal as well as take the opportunity to ask what you can do to resolve or improve the situation.

CASE 4
Layoffs and Terminations: The Company's Point of View

"Because of the lack of demand for products and the stiff competition we face, we have had to lay off a lot of employees this year," remarks Greg, a manager for a large auto manufacturing company. "It's tragic; all those eyes . . . scared and sad . . . and all that anger. . . ." He heaves a long sigh. "It really hits me in the gut, but we all know it has to be done. The company can't afford to pay them any more, so they might as well go out and find someone who can until our business gets back on track—if it ever will."

Jane, the owner of a medium-sized advertising agency, agrees with Greg that the process is just as painful for management as it is for the employees. "They expect us to give them security," she explains, "but in this industry, you can't count on anything—especially now, when advertisers are afraid to spend because consumers are afraid to buy. It's a big circle; people buy products, businesses can produce more, and people stay in their jobs because they're needed. That's why so many people are out of work now; there's no production because consumers don't have the money to spend because they don't have jobs. And so it goes."

Termination, says Chris, a manager at a record production studio, is also tough on those who hold the ax. "When you find you can't work with someone, or that they're not performing up to your and the client's expectations, there's nothing else you can do. And it hurts; it's a question on someone's efforts and capabilities. But the bottom line is that the job has to be done."

_____ CASE 5 _____

Labor Relations: When Your Boss Brings the Family into Business

"When my boss brought his wife into the business, it was all over for me and my staff," remembers Ray, a manager at a small pest-control company. "She started trying to control things, and she did because her husband, the owner, was blind to what she was doing and how it was hurting our sales. But it was what she wanted to do—run the business—and he had to give her the chance because he loved her. They started blaming the decrease in sales on me, and it was only a couple of months before they let me go. I think the rest of the staff quit not too long after because they couldn't stand the situation."

Like many employees of small or family-owned companies, Ray was pushed out by a relation of someone higher in power. "She didn't have the experience or the customer or product knowledge that I did," he says, "but that didn't matter, because as soon as she came into the business, her opinion held more weight than mine. My boss, the owner, wouldn't listen to my opinions or ideas any more, and when I questioned the way she ran things, he got angry. He thought I was jealous or something. Maybe I was, but I saw things going bad and I wanted to stop them; she just didn't know what she was doing and I wanted to teach her. But she wouldn't listen, either. When they let me go, they didn't even give me a reason. They just saw me as a troublemaker and wanted to get me out of there. And believe me, by that time, I was glad to go!"

_____ CASE 6 _____

Tools of the Trade: When You Can't Handle the Job

"I knew I shouldn't have accepted my last promotion," says Alison, an executive at a large publishing company. "I had only been with the company for a few years, and I knew it wasn't enough time. Everyone at that level was a lot older than me and knew the business inside out. I was flattered, so I took the position, but the more I tried, the worse the situation became."

Alison explains that because she didn't have the knowledge or experience of the others at her level, her opinions weren't valued by the other executives, and she quickly began making mistakes. "The harder I tried, the deeper I dug my grave," she admits. "I guess I was stubborn, too; I wanted to be this young star who could change things for the better, but I lacked the basics to make anything happen. So, when my boss walked in one afternoon and announced that I would no longer be working for the company, I wasn't surprised."

She mentions that she could have probably asked for a trial period in the position, or that she could have been more open to the suggestions of others and learn exactly what she was getting into. "I guess my ego got in the way," she laughs sadly. "I thought, 'They must have a lot of confidence in me to put me here.' And they did—but I should have known better. Some jobs are just too much. You have to understand the position and your full responsibilities before you take a new job."

_____ CASE 7 _____
Keeping Your Ear to the Ground

"This company keeps a tight lid on employee comings and goings," says Jim, a manager at a large retail store chain, "but I always have a scoop on things through the company grapevine. I need to keep in touch with the news because I have to know what my employees are doing, who's in trouble, what's bothering them, and so on. It gives me a jump on my staff and on changes that could affect my job and my future here."

The grapevine is what tipped him off to plans for a new store and saved him from losing his job at the one that closed down. "I have a connection in personnel, so when I heard the news, I immediately expressed interest in the position at the new store, before any other candidates were considered. By the time the company president made his announcement, I was first in their minds. A lot of people were swept away by my store's closing, though, because there weren't enough positions in other locations. If I hadn't known about it beforehand, I probably would have been caught in a tough situation, and I would have never secured the job I have here today."

3

Strategic Preparation: How to Walk the Plank without Getting Wet

When you're certain that unemployment is on the way, it helps to be prepared. So, what can you do?

AT WORK

Organize your facts. This means gathering all the notes you've put together about your job performance and value to the company to prove that you're too irreplaceable to be laid off, or that you don't deserve to be fired. In a layoff situation, the decisions are usually final, but in a few instances, employees who have pointed out their integral functions within the company have managed to hang onto their jobs. And, if you're in a termination situation, it helps to know where to find the answers to refute the questions and charges your employer might have against you.

Find out your company's termination procedure.

Talk to anyone you know who has been laid off or fired, even if it's Uncle Ed or your neighbor's daughter. Be discreet if you ask people in your own company, but definitely ask them. Stories of layoffs and terminations are some of the most popular to circulate through the gossip network.

Read through your employee manual.

There may be additional references that apply to your situation, such as the rules and reasons for layoffs and termination, and a rundown of the investigation process in general. Also, you may find a listing of your rights during the procedure, such as the right to have an attorney present, the right to take a cut in pay instead of losing your job, the right to have a lawyer examine your severance package, and the right to have the chance to resign. Some companies even have a disciplinary grievance system that allows you to make a complaint against any unfair actions and bring it for review before a board of company directors. For examples, see chart 3.1.

Find out which benefits are available and those to which you're entitled.

Use chart 3.2 to list the benefits you know your company offers, such as severance pay, compensation for unused vacation days, pension, and so on. Sometimes you can bargain for more, especially if you have been a valuable employee or you have been with the company for a long time. It never hurts to ask, because the worst they can do is say no.

Also, check on the status of your insurance. Most companies will extend your usual health benefits for a certain period of time after you've left them—for a hefty fee. For details on these programs, see chart 3.3.

To obtain a new health insurance plan with a new carrier, you will probably need a physical exam, so if you don't exercise regularly, start getting in shape. Some professional organizations offer individual insurance options, or you could obtain a spouse or family health insurance package through your wife's or husband's employer. Now is the time to find out what is available and what switching insurance plans involves on your part.

If you have stock in the company or are enrolled in a 401K plan, read your forms to find out your choices on handling your investments. Some companies will allow former employees to keep their stock; others will request that the stock be transferred to a different account outside of the company. Also, if you have money in the company credit union, you'll need to decide if you would like to pull it out and switch it to another bank, especially if the credit union offices are in the building of your former employer.

CHART 3.1

What Are Your Rights as an Employee?

Not all companies grant every one of these rights, and some will offer even more to their employees. Check your employee manual to find out which rights your company offers. Or, talk with someone in the personnel department.

- The right to examine your personnel file and question any notations you believe are biased or unfounded.

- The right to consult an attorney about your job loss situation, and bring him or her to the final interview, board hearings, and other meetings that involve and affect your employment status.

- The right to choose between resignation or termination.

- The right to choose outplacement services instead of or in addition to severance pay and benefits.

- The right to appeal any job loss decision to a higher board of company directors.

- The right to have several days between the time you receive the unemployment agreement and the time you sign it.

- The right to compete for any clients or accounts that came as a direct result of your work.

- The right to take with you any items to which you may have contributed (projects, documents, etc.).

- The right to examine all notations and evidence regarding your termination.

- The right to receive all back pay, bonuses, and unused vacation and sick days owed to you.

- The right to re-apply for work at the company when the industry picks up business.

CHART 3.2

Benefits Your Company Might Offer

Check on these options before you lose your job:

- Severance pay*

- Vacation pay

- Bonuses

- Health insurance

- Life insurance

- 401K plan

- Retirement/pension

- Tuition reimbursement (check whether full reimbursement applies if you're in the middle of a semester)

- Outplacement services or Employee Assistance Programs

- Stock

- Use of office space and equipment

- Good references

- Company car

- Secretarial/assistant services

*Make sure you get your severance agreement in writing!

CHART 3.3

Definition: The COBRA Plan

Under the Consolidated Omnibus Budget Reconciliation Act (COBRA), employees are able to continue their health benefits through their company plan beyond the date their employment was terminated. This coverage is optional and is available for a maximum of anywhere from six to eighteen months, depending on the individual state's law.

There are, however, some conditions of benefit continuation that you should be aware of before you enroll. These include:

- You are only allowed the decision to continue coverage under the plan in which you were participating on the day of your job termination.

- Coverage is only extended to employees who were covered at the time of termination.

- Your employer will not contribute to your coverage; the entire cost must be paid by you.

- This coverage ends on the first date any of the following conditions apply:
  -when your eligibility period ends
  -when your employer ceases to provide coverage under the plan to any employee
  -when you do not make your payment on time
  -when you are covered under another health plan
  -when you become eligible for Medicare

To receive this continued coverage, you will still have to re-enroll and complete new enrollment forms with the insurance company. Be sure to talk with your benefits coordinator or the company representative to find out the exact details of the plan for which you are eligible, the time of eligibility, and the cost. Then, check around for your options; you may find the costs much lower than continuing your company plan.

Make a notebook.

This is your "fight-back" book, which you are going to fill with questions to ask your employer during the layoff or termination interview, including points and demands you'd like to make during the negotiations. In it, you can refer to the benefits to which you're entitled, questions about the company's future, possibilities for being re-hired, health plans, reasons you are valuable to your employer, and encouraging notes to yourself. There are also negotiable "extras" many laid-off and fired employees usually do not think to ask for, such as references, office space, and use of equipment. See chart 3.4 for examples.

Clean up your desk or office.

If you're sure you're leaving, there's no sense in staying around longer than you have to. Put your files in order for easy access, along with everything else you will want to take with you when you leave. Put all the files and papers that have to stay in order for the next person, and make a list of pending projects that someone else will need to finish when you're gone. Check them off as you finish them if several days or weeks pass before you leave. It's just good business. And, if anyone asks why you're putting everything in order, just say you're cleaning house.

Leave a great impression.

Make the rounds of your office—cheerful disposition and smile intact—and say hello to everyone every day you're still there. Ask your co-workers how they are, how their jobs are going, and thank them for helping you with a specific project or task. It's the last thing you'll feel like doing, but the results are great for your confidence; you'll realize how much you did for others and how much everyone really does appreciate your efforts on the job. Also, you'll leave a lasting impression of confidence, competence, and warmth with your company that will be hard to forget—and one that leaves you with many people who will be willing to help you, even give you references, in the future.

AT HOME
Write a new resume and general cover letter.

After you've been laid off or fired, you'll be much too shaken to do this. Right now you have the anger and determination to make it an excellent

CHART 3.4

Your "Fight-Back" Book

If you think you might soon find yourself in a termination or layoff meeting, this is an essential tool to have with you. Inside a notebook, write down these questions, and any others you can think of—or take this sheet with you and make notations during the final interview. This will help you remember all the things you need to ask, as well as act as proof of your employer's concessions and reasoning during the process.

Don't forget—ask for all terms of agreement in writing!

Questions to ask your employer during the final meeting:

1. Why exactly am I being laid off or fired?

   _____

2. What are my benefits?

   _____

3. How much severance pay will I receive?

   _____

4. Does this decision have anything to do with my job performance?

   _____

5. Will you provide me with a good reference when I apply for work?

   _____

6. Do I have to leave the building today? If not, how long can I use my office, the equipment, assistants, company car, and so on?

   _____

continued

7. What type of health-care options do I have, and who can explain them?

_____

8. What is the status of this company (if you're being laid off)? Will it close? Is there a merger in sight?

_____

9. Is there a chance I will be re-hired when profits and productivity rise in the future?

_____

10. Do you have any suggestions or recommendations of people or companies who might be looking for a worker with my qualifications?

_____

11.

_____

12.

_____

13.

_____

14.

_____

15.

_____

16.

_____

17.

_____

tool for future employment. Write your resume as if you have left the company and you are looking for broader horizons: You are. So, look beyond the point you're at now and get your credentials down. Ask your friends and family for help, if you need it. When the ax falls, it will take you a while to bounce back, but when you do, your ready-made cover letter and resume will give you confidence and a new sense of purpose. For a few ideas on how to write a resume and cover letter, check out the list in chart 3.5.

List all of your potential job contacts.

This could take a while, so start writing down people you know in your field, at your level or higher. Then, branch out into areas you might consider for employment in the future. For example, if you have an interest in gardening, would there be a position for you in a biological research firm, a natural park, or a civic center? If you love to travel, how about airlines, agencies, publications, or hotels? Get the idea? Now, turn to chart 3.6 and list everyone you know who could provide you with information and help you with your career.

Get your finances in order.

Using the budget chart (chart 3.7), list your assets—what you have in cash and what you own—and your liabilities—what you owe or expect to pay as monthly bills and unplanned expenses. You may feel too muddled to do this after you've been laid off or fired. So in the meantime, use your nervous energy to get your expenses in order. *Now*.

Explore your options.

Maybe you've always wanted to take a few months off to write, paint, or find your hidden skills. Perhaps you've always dreamed of traveling, or you'd like to explore fields other than your own. Would you like to finish that college degree, for which you have been trying to find the time for the last decade? How about earning your master's degree, or your Ph.D.?

Use chart 3.8 to list all the skills you have, on or off the job. Don't be shy (we've provided some ideas to start you off), and use your family or friends to help you brainstorm. Remember, have fun! When your job is gone, you will have the opportunity to do many of the things you couldn't have considered otherwise, because with the loss of employment come the gifts of time and freedom.

CHART 3.5

Resume and Cover Letter Resources

How to Write a Winning Resume
(Deborah Perlmutter Bloch, VGM Career Horizons)

The Perfect Resume
(Tom Jackson, Doubleday)

The Resume Kit
(Richard H. Beatty, John Wiley & Sons, Inc.)

Resumes for Better Jobs
(ARCO)

Resumes That Knock 'Em Dead
(Martin John Yate, Bob Adams, Inc.)

Career resources

VGM Career Books (also published by VGM Career Horizons)
  How to Make the Right Career Moves
  How to Change Your Career
  Joyce Lain Kennedy's Career Book
  Life Plan
  Planning Your Career of Tomorrow
  Careers Encyclopedia
  Occupational Outlook Handbook
  "Opportunities in . . ." (e.g.: accounting, dance, law, medical technology, telecommunications, and so on), career series.

Additional career resources

How to Locate Jobs and Land Interviews
(Albert French, Career Press)

Jobs!
(Robert O. Snelling, Sr. and Anne M. Snelling, Fireside Books)

Taking Charge of Your Career
(Kiplinger Books)

CHART 3.6

List Your Potential Contacts

Name	Title/Company	Field
_____	_____	_____
_____	_____	_____
_____	_____	_____
_____	_____	_____
_____	_____	_____
_____	_____	_____
_____	_____	_____
_____	_____	_____
_____	_____	_____
_____	_____	_____
_____	_____	_____
_____	_____	_____
_____	_____	_____
_____	_____	_____
_____	_____	_____
_____	_____	_____

CHART 3.7

Budget Chart

Your assets	Value	Your debts	Monthly bills	Payments
House	$_____	$_____	Rent/Mortgage	$_____
Car	$_____	$_____	Vehicles	$_____
Savings	$_____		Utilities	$_____
401K	$_____		Loans	$_____
Pension	$_____		Food	$_____
Severance pay (estimated)	$_____		Transportation	$_____
Vacation pay (estimated)	$_____		Extras	$_____
Other	$_____	$_____	Other	$_____
	$_____	$_____		$_____
	$_____	$_____		$_____
	$_____	$_____		$_____
	$_____	$_____		$_____

Totals: $_____ $_____ $_____
Assets   Debts   Bills

CHART 3.8

List Your Skills

These are just a few ideas to get you started. Fill in the blanks with more!

On the job:	Additional activities:	Untapped skills:
Good leader	Enjoy physical activity	Musical talent
Good speaker	Like to create, build	Mathematical ability
Work well with others	Computer tasks	Have eye for design
Enjoy challenges	Like working with hands	Artistic talent
Like to supervise	Planning and research	Writing skills
_____	_____	_____
_____	_____	_____
_____	_____	_____
_____	_____	_____
_____	_____	_____
_____	_____	_____
_____	_____	_____
_____	_____	_____
_____	_____	_____
_____	_____	_____

continued

On the job: **Additional activities:**   **Untapped skills:**

CHART 3.9

What Have You Dreamed of Doing with Your Life?

- Own your own business?
- Work with children?
- Travel?

- Write a cookbook?
- Learn another language?
- Finish your degree?

- Enter a contest?
- Work with animals?
- Sell your artwork?

Career fantasies:

_____

_____

_____

_____

_____

_____

_____

_____

_____

_____

_____

Other dreams:

_____

_____

_____

_____

_____

_____

_____

_____

_____

_____

_____

CASE 8

Methods of Madness: How the Ax Can Fall

"We've had three layoffs—massive layoffs—since I came to this company five years ago," says Sam, an employee at a large manufacturing company. "It's almost spooky the way management does it, too; they don't tell anyone that it's going to happen. They just call different people into their offices for meetings on Friday afternoon and then everyone starts packing up, very quietly, without saying a word. We dread the end of the week now; we're not looking forward to another 'Black Friday.' It's the luck of the draw who goes and who survives."

Jennifer, a manager at a nationally known machine production company, has a different story to tell. "When they conducted the last layoff here, the company brought everybody into the auditorium and told us what was going on," she remembers. "They were very open about it and answered our questions, but then came the kicker. They told us that when we returned to our desks, we would find an envelope announcing whether or not we were still employed. I was so furious that I didn't even open mine. I figured if they were going to get rid of me, they were going to have to at least have the guts to tell me to my face."

Remembers Tony, an executive at a large grocery store chain, "They let us all go at noon, on a cold Friday in January. There we were, three hundred of us, walking down the street carrying our boxes of personal supplies, like some sort of crazy parade. We were all so stunned we didn't even feel the cold. They had simply called us all together and announced the departments that were closing. Then we met with our managers and collected our things. It was funny though; all I could think was that I was glad they let us go early, so I could get back and figure things out before my wife came home."

Says Stacy, a production manager for a small advertising agency, "There was only one other person laid off when I was, and we took it about the same. The agency owner called us into his office at 4:30 on a Friday and told us he didn't need our services any more; he couldn't afford them, really. He was very apologetic, but it didn't do anything to kill the pain and anger I felt. My God, I'm raising two kids by myself, and the least he could have done was give me a chance to look around when he realized things were getting bad. As it was, I had no indication whatsoever that it was coming."

Peter, a college student and former waiter, also was caught by surprise. "The restaurant told me they would call me because they didn't have the work schedule finalized," he says. "I waited for days because I had to buy books for the semester . . . but they never called."

———————— CASE 9 ————————
Termination: When It Hits You by Surprise

"I couldn't believe it when I was fired," exclaims Sandy, the former publicist for an education center. "It was such an unbelievable situation; the boss was having an affair with his secretary, and he decided he wanted to bring her into my position. I got a great severance deal because I was able to bargain with him. He paid me a lot of money to keep the situation under the table, because if the institution found out, it would be his job. But I think he knew I was afraid to tell them about his affair; after all, what could they do, really? And besides, who would believe me? My boss had a lot more clout than I did, so I decided not to push it. Now that I think back on it, it was stupid not to, but I was young. What could I do?"

Says Tom, a copywriter for a large advertising firm, "When I was fired, it was completely unfair. I was accused of doing something I didn't, but nobody even told me there was a problem until they had me in the final meeting. I would have been able to explain my side of it, but no one was listening at that point." He pounds his fist angrily on the table. "It was a simple miscommunication, or a misunderstanding, but suddenly I was a pariah and no one cared what I had to say."

"I know my new boss and I didn't get along," recalls Lila, a producer at a local radio station. "But I was really trying to see things her way, and to help her learn about our listeners. There was a lot she didn't know, but she didn't want to hear it from me, a lowly producer. There was a lot of conflict between us in the end, because I also didn't think it was fair that I had to change my style at her whim when I had been there eight years. But I never thought it would come to being fired. Never."

Explains Ken, a sales account representative for a large publication, "OK, so my sales weren't as high as they could have been, but they weren't the lowest, by far. Maybe I was too aggressive. Maybe I was too competitive. Maybe I was too willing to bend rules to get a sale. I don't know. I got desperate, finally, but I always thought things would get better. When they fired me, it knocked the wind out of me. I couldn't even say anything, I was so shocked." He shook his head in wonder. "And you know, it still really hurts, more than six months later."

"I didn't think they could get rid of me," smiles Carolyn, a former manager for a bookstore chain. "I knew I'd screwed up on something, but I was valuable in so many other ways. The company needed me, I thought. But when I brought it up in the meeting, they told me they'd just train somebody else. I guess that's the way it works in every company, though; there's always someone else somewhere who has the potential to be as good at or better at your job than you."

Arnold, a buyer for a department store, remembers, "At my last job, I made a big error that I was afraid to admit. So I didn't, and it multiplied into a catastrophe that cost the company a lot of money. They had no choice but to punish me," he admits. "If only I had told someone about it."

4

The Final Confrontation:
Turning Termination to Your Advantage

You're gathered in an auditorium with the company president and hundreds of fellow workers, or you're in a meeting room with a few other employees, or it's just you and your boss alone in the office behind closed doors. In each of these scenes, there are many similarities; the room is silent with tension, and each person is filled with dread as he or she waits for the bad news to be delivered. You know what it means; your employment with the company has ended. But if you haven't been in the situation before, what can you really expect to hear?

WHEN IS THE BAD NEWS DELIVERED?

According to experts in job counseling and company personnel departments, the best time for businesses to give employees the news of layoffs or terminations is early in the day and early in the week. This way employees have time to collect their belongings and get their emotions to-

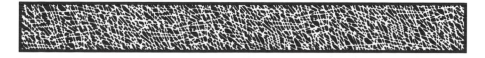

gether, as well as wrap up their duties and say goodbye. The beginning of the work week is also better because employees can jump right into the job search without losing momentum. This prevents workers from slipping into shock during the delay time that is created, which sends many of those who lose their jobs on Friday or before a long holiday into a depression from which it is hard to escape.

However, the reality is that most employers still prefer to stall layoffs and terminations until the end of the day and, yes, the end of the week. The theory is that it protects the employee from the embarrassment of walking through the offices and collecting his or her belongings in front of now former coworkers. When held late on Friday, layoffs and terminations are actually more advantageous to the employer, who doesn't have to worry as much about disgruntled workers acting up or lashing out in anger at others in the company. It is also a procedure that seems like more of a true ending for all parties involved, and supposedly, it gives the employee the weekend to cool off and think about his or her options.

WHO GIVES THE BAD NEWS?

The more people who are losing their jobs, the more powerful the person who is appointed to deliver the news. When a large corporation lays off thousands of employees, for instance, the president or CEO might handle the announcement, for reasons of publicity as well as to make an appearance for confidence in the stability of the company. Smaller businesses that are terminating several people might choose the department manager or director to tell the employees, while a singular termination might involve only the immediate manager. In most cases someone from the company's human resources or personnel department also will attend the meeting to act as a witness and a mediator.

WHERE IS THE BAD NEWS GIVEN?

For widespread layoffs, you'll usually be gathered with all other employees targeted for pink-slip treatment, perhaps in an auditorium or large assembly hall. For single layoffs, employers will try to choose a neutral area, such as a meeting room or a superior's office, something to make the incident as calm and bland as possible, and to give the employee a nonvolatile environment in which to absorb and accept the news. Employers also want to deliver the news somewhere quiet, without distracting noises or interruptions.

WHAT YOUR EMPLOYER CAN OFFER YOU
Layoffs

Making massive cutbacks is one of the worst things an employer ever has to do. Putting large numbers of people out of work—tens, hundreds, or even thousands—for an unknown amount of time, and jeopardizing their family security and career future, is a horrible experience no matter how necessary the action might be. And for you, the employee, it is nothing less than frightening to lose your financial security, your family of coworkers, and your work identity.

At larger companies, when layoffs occur, the employees are usually gathered in one large area, and the company president or another high-ranking official will take charge of the situation, explaining the company's financial status, the current economy of the industry, any changes in profits and technology, or whatever other reasons might have caused the decision to cut back on staff. In a smaller company, there may be only one or two employees who are confronted with a layoff situation, but the procedure is very much the same; your manager, someone from personnel, or the company president informs you of the need to place your employment on hold due to corporate factors, industry climate, business debt, technology, and so on.

The company's goal is to first help you understand *why* you are being laid off from your job, and then show you options for your employment future, offering assistance to help you get back on your feet. Some choices employers may offer instead of complete job loss can include:

- Cutbacks in salary or hourly pay

- Cutbacks in work hours

- Upgraded severance packages in exchange for leaving

- Cutbacks in overtime and bonuses

- Asking for volunteers to take the layoff option

- Offering early retirement to qualified employees

- Offering transfers to another office or branch of the company

If you are given one or more of these options, or any others, make sure you ask for time to make your choice. Don't decide right away. Discuss the matter with fellow employees, your family, even your friends, to get their feedback. The suggestions that turn up may surprise you, even if you think you know what you want during the meeting.

Larger employers—and many small companies—often have outplacement services ready to provide employees with counseling, job advice, retraining and skill classes, resume services, interview help, and job placement assistance after the layoffs occur. If this type of service is available through your company, look into it carefully before you decide to use it. Many companies will offer outplacement services for free; if so, by all means take advantage of the valuable help it can offer you in regaining confidence, reworking your credentials, and finding a new job. Other businesses, however, offer outplacement in exchange for other benefits, namely severance pay or any type of monetary bonus that might be received as an incentive to cooperate with the layoff.

If outplacement is offered in exchange for something else, take a good look at your job prospects before you choose to give up your money or other benefits. You may already be prepared for another position, with your resume, portfolio, and contacts updated. Or, you may be in a field that has a growing demand for workers with your qualifications and with other companies poised to make you an offer.

Whatever you do, don't allow yourself to be hastened into making a decision about anything. You're under a lot of pressure; perhaps you need to consult with others, such as your family, before you decide what to do. The best plan is to find out your company's layoff policies, procedures, and outplacement services ahead of time so you can examine your choices before you find yourself in that silent, tension-filled room with the company "ax" man or woman, cringing as you listen to the news.

Firing

"Could you come into my office, please? There's something I need to talk to you about."

That's the classic opening bid for termination, the calm request that doesn't even hint at the trouble that lies beneath it. It could happen in the morning, or any day of the week, but most likely, it will occur late Friday afternoon, or on the afternoon of the day you are usually paid.

You'll walk, unsuspecting, into the cold, angry office, where other managers or someone from personnel may be waiting as well, notepads full of reasons and evidence balanced on their laps, a mix of sorrow and relief in their eyes. Their voices will be almost too calm in an effort to keep you from blazing up in anger or fear. But you're going to be prepared for this, your mind strong, your emotions cool, and your "fight-back" notebook of questions and rebuttals ready.

If you weren't told the purpose of this meeting and you suddenly discover you're being terminated, excuse yourself to go get your notebook of questions now. They'll let you go. Your employer, believe it or not, wants to help you as much as possible right *now*, so they can prove they made everything clear to you during the exit interview, immediately diffusing as many of your worries as possible to avoid problems and conflict after you have walked out the door for the last time.

You may be given the option to resign first. This is often supposedly a choice that offers you the chance to "save face." Well, think about it, long and hard, because resigning prevents you from receiving valuable unemployment benefits you may need (see chapter 8). In addition, most people realize that in some fields, resigning is just a synonym for firing. Things to ask can include whether you can get a good reference from your company, what their reference policy is, and what will happen if you don't resign. If could be a bluff to get rid of you. Do not be afraid to ask questions!

For the most part, employers like to keep the layoff and termination procedures simple—just you, your manager, and anyone else involved (unless the numbers are massive) in a quiet, if possible peaceful, office area. The atmosphere will be tense, to say the least; you're angry at them, possibly even at yourself, for taking away your job security, and your employer is worrying about the effect the discharge will have on you. Will you break down? Go crazy? Scream and threaten them? Punch someone in your anger?

These are all very real fears the person breaking the news to you holds in his or her mind, but don't give them the satisfaction of acting like a child and proving to them that you deserve the job loss by letting go of your emotions. Instead, remain calm, professional, and prepared. Read chart 4.1 for some suggestions on how to hold on to your inner feelings and stay strong during the final meeting, leaving a positive last impression that could work for you in the future.

No matter what the scenario, however, your company has certain goals in mind when telling its employees about the situation, including:

- Clear communication of the reasons behind the layoff or termination

- An understanding that the employees are valued, appreciated, and will be provided for in the best means possible

- Avoiding or diffusing negative reactions and emotions by answering as many questions as possible and working through employee anxiety

- Offering solid options for the employee's future

When you have heard the news and know your options, the most important thing you can do is to listen closely and ask questions. If you don't understand something, ask about it. If you don't do it now, the company will assume that you do understand and you won't get the chance to ask again. Bring your checklist from the previous chapter, or your notebook of individual questions, along with a pen to write down comments as your employer talks so you can remember the things you want to ask about and need them to explain. Don't forget to ask about benefits as well, and don't be afraid to bring up any areas that aren't mentioned in your employer's initial announcement.

By preparing for the layoff or termination situation, you can walk away with more severance pay, special services, and a good set of references, far more than if you had come to the meeting uninformed, pas-

CHART ·4.1

Remaining Calm During the Final Interview

- Take several deep breaths.

- Ask if you can get a glass of water.

- Take your time when you answer and ask questions.

- Think about your family and the importance of how you handle this meeting, in terms of its impact on your future.

- Stand up and pace or walk around the room if you have to.

- Ask if you can have a moment of privacy alone in the office or room.

- Bring tissues.

- Don't forget your notebook. If your emotions start to get the better of you, you can always look down at it as if you were reading notations.

- If you're really upset, go ahead and ask for a day or so to calm down. If it isn't granted, leave anyway. You'll feel better and the meeting will go more smoothly for everyone once you have your emotions and thoughts together.

---

sive, and empty-handed. That's what your company expects, but you *deserve* the best benefits they have to offer, so bring your questions, ask them, and demand explanations. Your company should be willing to oblige.

When the day of layoffs or termination arrives, your employer will have all the paperwork prepared beforehand, complete with last paychecks, severance pay, final statements, and work releases, all ready except for your signature. *Important point:* If you have any questions about anything, DON'T SIGN ANY PAPERS! Instead, ask for time to talk with a lawyer, or to make a phone call if you already have a lawyer and would like him or her to examine the provisions for fairness and accuracy.

This doesn't mean you distrust your employer or that you're going behind your company's back. You no longer have a commitment to your company, remember? Or, rather, they no longer have a commitment to you, so they're going to discourage any legal consultation, regardless of whether they have provided you with the severance package you deserve.

You may simply need time to talk with your family about the situation, for a reassuring ear if no other reason. You don't have to sit back and take what they give you right away; you deserve to know all your options, and you deserve time to think about it. Ultimately, you need to remember that you are in control of the situation, and you can ask or do anything you feel is right, including making a phone call or walking out and getting a second opinion. See case 11 for an example of a woman who did this and succeeded.

DO YOU NEED LEGAL COUNSEL?

Some companies have a standard layoff and termination procedure, so if you're aware of your employer's usual process and they're following it closely, or if there are a lot of workers being laid off, or if you're fairly new and have little time and energy invested in your employer, you probably don't have need for legal counsel. If, however, you're being laid off or fired in unusual circumstances, or if you feel you're not getting a fair deal, or if you're a minority or handicapped, or if your employer is avoiding questions and pressuring you . . . it might not hurt to ask a lawyer about the situation.

If you already have a lawyer, he or she can either give you advice or recommend you to a more qualified legal source who deals closely with corporate layoffs and termination. For more ideas, or if you don't have a lawyer, some inexpensive options to consider are listed in chart 4.2. And, if you're sure that your job is on the line, you may want to give them a call even before you lose your employment, to answer your questions, calm your fears, and let them know you may be needing their services soon.

PRESSURE SITUATIONS

The situation to watch out for during layoffs and terminations is when your employer brushes off your questions or tries to speed the meeting along in order to get you to sign the papers and shove you out the door. What can you do if you feel the pressure?

1. **Remain strong.** This is *your* life, *your* loss of employment, and you deserve to have answers and explanations. Not tomorrow, not Monday,

CHART 4.2

Where to Look for a Lawyer

- Local bar association

- Lawyer referral services

- Employment bureau recommendation

- Local college or university

- Professional associations and clubs

- Yellow Pages

- Friend or family referral

---

not next week, and not in a written request. It means *now*, face to face. And don't be afraid to stand your ground.

2. **Take your time.** If you feel you're being rushed or pressured to get through the termination process and sign the papers, *slow down and think.* You're going to be angry and confused and full of bitterness, but take a deep breath and remember the things you need to know. Since many companies will conduct their layoffs and terminations the last thing on Friday, they have an interest in getting things wrapped up quickly, and the sooner you're out of the building, the sooner they can stop worrying about your reactions and go home. So slow down, tell them you have a lot of things on your mind, and that you're not leaving until you're satisfied. Period. Your employer doesn't want to be there all night, and once he or she realizes you're not budging until you get some answers, they'll start talking.

3. **Don't let them pressure you.** Case 12 is an excellent example of an employee who stood her ground—and you *must* do the same. There is no reason to be afraid or guilty about it. Your employer is there to help you get through the painful process, and most companies will try to help you as much as possible, no matter how much time it takes. If you have to, walk out, there's no law against it. After consulting with others, even

a lawyer, and everyone is calm again, chances are that things will be resolved more smoothly.

4. **Bring your notebook.** Not only will this act as a cue card for the questions you need to ask, but it is also useful for writing down certain points you'll need to remember—facts that can be especially important when it comes to rehiring or claiming unemployment. If you can document that your employer said he or she would place you on the rehiring list when business picks up, or that your termination had nothing to do with illegal activities, you have proof that could get your position back in a better economy or provide you with unemployment funds that might have otherwise been questioned.

YOUR EXIT AND BEYOND

When everything has been settled and your papers have been signed, you want to leave a last impression that is professional, calm, and collected, no matter what you're feeling inside. How do you do it?

You do it in the following ways:

- Thank your employer for providing you with the years of employment and the income, and for giving you the chance to learn as much as you did.

- Hold back your emotions. Think of anything else but how you feel until you get outside the building. Make your attitude brisk and businesslike to avoid losing control.

- Shake hands, if you can.

- Then get out, quickly, and don't look back.

After the meeting ends, you probably won't have time to talk to or say goodbye to your fellow employees, unless it's a large layoff. Your employer wants you to leave the building as quickly as possible to avoid any theft, sabotage, or damage to company property, or any unprofessional reactions in front of other employees. You may be given a box or two in which to collect your things, with your manager or a third party watching you closely. Hopefully, you followed the advice in chapters 1 and 2 by cleaning out your important files and papers before the ax fell, making your final moments at your desk fewer and easier.

Take a good look around your office or area before you leave. What will you really miss about the job? Who did you really work well with, and who did you dislike? What did you accomplish? What did you learn? And, did you complete all the goals you had hoped for?

Keep these ideas in mind as you leave, for they will help shape the position and career you take next, as well as your direction for the future. But don't linger in your office; your time there, your job there, and your life there is over.

And now it's time to move on to better things!

_____ CASE 10 _____
Controlling the Final Meeting: When Your Emotions Get the Best of You

"When they told me I was no longer employed at the company, I just burst into tears," says Maria, a secretary for a large corporation. "All I could think of was that I was a failure, that I was too dumb and incapable of anything to hold onto my job. Oh, I was so upset I couldn't breathe, they kept telling me to calm down but I couldn't, I just lost control of everything. I finally asked if I could go to the restroom and get myself together but my boss wouldn't let me. He wanted to get it over with, I think. So, I just opened the door and ran out anyway. When I came back the next morning and apologized, I had all my priorities in order and I was ready to talk about options. Believe me, it went a lot smoother the second time around."

"I was very, very upset when my boss called me in his office and told me he had to let me go because I wasn't performing up to standard," remembers Bob, an auto mechanic. "I just thought, 'God, I've really busted my rear to learn all this stuff, and I've given a lot of years to my job.' Just because I was having a bad month or two wasn't a reason to get rid of me. I was going through a divorce and I was pretty upset, so it probably did affect my job. But when he told me, I was so angry I was afraid I'd punch him, so I got out of there for a couple hours. When I came back, we worked things out OK."

_____ CASE 11 _____
Controlling the Final Meeting: When to Walk Away

"When I was told of my termination, they just handed me this paper and expected me to sign," says Cindy, a writer for a small magazine. "I looked at them and said, 'Ha ha. You're not going to win that easily!' Then I walked out and took it to a lawyer, who was able to convince the magazine that, since I had been employed there for fifteen years and I had an excellent work record, that I deserved more compensation. So I got it. And it felt good."

"If only I had walked away," admits Lynne, a designer who had been with her firm just over two years. "But I was so surprised, and so scared. My boss really intimidated me. He just gave me the news, at 5:00, no less, and thundered at me to sign the agreement of terms. I tried to ask a few questions, but he kept yelling, 'Just sign it!' as if I was really stupid for even questioning him. How was I supposed to know I could have walked away until we were all more calm and I could have had some questions answered. I guess I felt that since I was being let go, there must be something wrong with me, and I deserved to be treated that way, like a stupid kid who didn't know anything. Well, now I've learned my lesson, and if it happens again, I'm walking away until I get answers and an agreement I can live with."

_____ CASE 12 _____
Standing Your Ground

"My boss called me into the director's office one Friday afternoon to 'discuss something' with me," explains Ria, an electrical engineer. "They told me they had some problems with my work and my actions—I'm very strong-minded—and they asked me if I would like to resign. I said, 'Wait a minute!' and ran to get my employee manual to look up the proper procedure before I went back to the office.

"Then," she continues, "I asked them for the exact reasons I was being asked to leave, and they wouldn't tell me anything, so I just stood there and said I wasn't budging until I got some answers. At the time, it was after five, and they just wanted to get out of there, I could tell. After five minutes of silence, they started to talk. And I found out it wasn't the quality of my work that was bugging them, but rather the way I didn't play the corporate game. They didn't say it in so many words, but basically, I don't kiss up to the partners the way everyone else did around there. I had my own mind and my own ideas and I wasn't afraid to throw out alternatives. They took that as a play for control."

Ria adds that she chose not to resign, thinking it was a bluff, but her boss then told her that her employment was terminated at the company. "They handed me this paper stating the severance terms and the reason, but I just couldn't sign it," she says. "After another half hour of arguing that it wasn't fair, I did sign it, but I added my own explanation underneath. I wanted to make the final record clear."

5

Your First Hours of Freedom:
What to Do, Where to Go, and Ways to Handle the Panic

You have cleaned out your office. You have said goodbye to your coworkers, if allowed. You have taken a last look around. You have walked out of the building. What now?

Beneath all the emotions you're feeling, under the anger and sadness and betrayal and hurt, there's probably a huge bubble of emptiness. Where will you find a new job? How will you pay the bills? Who can you talk to? Will they understand? A thousand questions are running through your mind, but you aren't sure of the direction in which your next step should be . . . until now.

First, let's go over what you won't do:

1. **You won't let your emotions control you.** You won't rant and rave and scream and curse out everyone you see. You also won't let your anger cause you to damage any person or property, verbally or physically, at your former company. Not only is it unprofessional, dangerous, and crazy, it can also land you in jail. Get outside and move on.

2. **You won't plot revenge.** You're angry, and you feel betrayed and hurt, but it's *over*. Your job is gone. Don't waste your time and energy thinking about retribution tactics because it's useless. Besides, you're smarter than that. You know revenge will only get you into more trouble, and thinking about it isn't going to make your life better or get back your

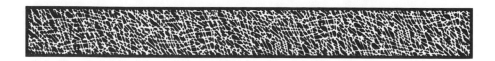

job. And, the best revenge is getting a future job that gives you more happiness, benefits, and security than the one you just left. So forget about revenge and think instead about what you really want from your life in the future.

3. **You won't damage company property**. Tempting as it may seem to trash files, erase computer documents, and rip up previous work—DON'T! A violent exit will only give you even greater problems with your former company, and right now the only thing you need to do is to get away from them. Don't even think about it; make your exit calm, professional, legal, and *final*.

4. **You won't look back**. "I should have said this." "I could have done that." "If only this would have happened . . . I'd still have my job!"

You're probably thinking along these lines, but you can't change the past. If layoffs were coming, it's hardly your fault your job is gone. If you were fired, there was most likely a just cause for it; and if not, someone obviously wasn't going to give you a second chance anyway.

This is a turning point in your life, and though it really hurts, realize that your new life is beginning. So chuck your "could have," "should have," and "would have" phrases aside and get started on future thinking!

5. **You won't become desperate**. Remember, you have only lost your job, not your life, and your life is the most valuable thing you have. Within you, there is the potential to do *anything*: save lives, change minds, start a business, forward technology, and, most importantly, run your own show. *You* are in control. And you can do anything you believe you can.

You only live once, and life is a gift. Now is your time to use it in the way that *you* choose, and to choose to do what gives *you* the most satisfaction and fulfillment.

This means you won't go out and get drunk or drugged. Losing your job is just an excuse, and now is your time to be strong. You need to feel this pain, not delay it. And you won't even think about taking your life, because, face it, your job is not all there is to being alive.

NOW, WHAT DO I DO?

1. **Go somewhere quiet where you can sit alone and think**.

Before you confront friends, family, and future job prospects, you need to get your mind and emotions together. You will have to face your own thoughts and feelings about your job loss first, and work through them alone. This will not only help you become calm and bounce back with hope more quickly, but it will also prevent you from taking out those feelings on the ones you love. A few good, quiet, private places to think about going include the library, a park, or a home office.

Don't bother going to a bar; the temptation to drown your pain may turn out to be too great. Remember, you'll need a clear head to think through your emotions and to break the news to the ones you love.

CHART 5.1

The Final Confrontation

Fill in the answers to the following questions about your final meeting or termination interview. Add the details as you remember them.

1. Reason for layoff/termination: _____

2. Benefits offered and their amounts:

   Severance pay: _____   Other: _____

   Unused vacation: _____   _____

   Stock: _____   _____

   401K or pension: _____   _____

   Bonus: _____   _____

3. Health plan and insurance options: _____

   _____

   _____

4. Who announced the layoff/termination? _____

5. Were you the only one? _____ How many others? _____

6. How did everyone act toward you? _____

   _____

7. Did anyone get out of hand? _____

   _____

8. Give a brief summary of the meeting, including your employer's reactions, your thoughts, how you felt, and whether you believe you were treated fairly.

_____

_____

_____

_____

_____

_____

_____

9. Write down any other details or questions that stand out in your mind.

_____

_____

_____

_____

_____

_____

_____

CHART 5.2

What Are Your Feelings?

Check off the emotions you're feeling now, just after losing your job. Then
fill in the reasons why you feel this way in the space below.

☐ Fear

_____

_____

_____

☐ Sadness

_____

_____

_____

☐ Excitement

_____

_____

_____

☐ Shame

_____

_____

_____

☐ Anger

_____

_____

_____

☐ Betrayal

_____

_____

_____

☐ Relief

_____

_____

_____

☐ Hurt

_____

_____

_____

CHART 5.3

Working Out Your Emotions

- **Keep a daily journal** of your thoughts and feelings, and keep it with you all the time. That way, when you're in line at the store, or at the gym, or on the bus, or just walking to an appointment, you have a good, quiet way of letting out your emotions.

- **"Work out" your feelings**. When you feel angry, sad, anxious, or depressed, go for a run, do twenty-five sit-ups, dance to the radio, or take a brisk walk. This physical activity will trigger positive endorphins in your brain to control your negative feelings and make you feel better, as well as do something good for your body.

- **Talk, talk, talk**. Keep a close network of friends and family with whom you can talk every day, or at least when you're feeling down. Or, talk to yourself; you can—and should be—your own best friend.

- **Express your emotions creatively**. Draw or sketch out your feelings with colors or in a cartoon. Make up new words to a popular song you know and sing out your emotions. Write a poem about it, or a short story. Put your feelings to work in your hobby, or even take up a new craft for enjoyable therapy.

---

2. **Write down everything you can remember about the final meeting.**

Fill out the questions on chart 5.1 and use the rest of the space to add in the details. This will help you make a case for getting your job back should the industry pick up, or to receive unemployment benefits if your employer contests your claim. And, it will be useful later on, when you can look back on the reasons, and either change your own life through what you have learned, or help others through your experience.

3. **Let yourself feel the loss.**

The sooner you realize and accept the fact that you won't be going back to your old desk, in your old office, in your old building on Monday, the sooner you'll treat it as part of your past and be ready to move ahead to a better, more fulfilling life.

CHART 5.4

Forget Your Stress

- Get out with friends

- See a movie

- Listen to music you love

- Exercise

- Get out to a park or a recreational area and enjoy your freedom

- Read a classic book you enjoy

- Go to a museum you have always wanted to visit

- Try the symphony, a play, or something new that will give you an enjoyable experience

- Take a warm bath by candlelight

- Go to a spa, or get a massage

- Rent hilarious movies and laugh, laugh, laugh!

---

4. **Get out those emotions**.

Use the list in chart 5.2 to examine your feelings about the loss of your job. Some of the most common reactions are listed, but write in your own as you think of them and fill in the reasons why.

If you're really alone, or when you're alone later, get it out of your system; cry, pound your fist on your knee, wrinkle your face up, or scream into a pillow. Whatever you do, get those emotions out as soon as you can when you feel them during the weeks to come. Don't hold them back inside because, like all humans, when you shove your feelings down deep, they appear in other strange ways: in your actions and attitudes, and in the words you write and speak.

Sometimes, when you are talking with a prospective employer, those emotions can pop out of nowhere if they're still in your heart, turning the interviewer off and leaving a negative image of you in his or her mind. Get those feelings out now so you can make a fresh start on your new life without that old baggage. Look at chart 5.3 for ways to work out the emotions you're feeling in the weeks to come.

5. **And now, calm down.**

Right, you scoff, I just lost my job, my income, my security, and my life! Well, if you've worked through your emotions, you're probably down to the emptiness stage, or at least you're somewhat more calm.

That's good. It isn't time to worry about what you're going to do, about money, or about the future. Now it's time to try and relax, to let your mind go, and to do something good for you.

You're probably not thinking very clearly right now, so chart 5.4 lists a few suggestions of activities that will relax you and get your mind off the stress of losing your job. You probably won't have a lot of fun, but try to laugh, or to do something that makes you really happy. Why? Because:

- You are in control of your life.

- Your job is no longer your life.

- Your future is up to *you*.

- And you can be as happy as you want to be!

Make the decision to be good to yourself, and to look for opportunities to change your life for the better. Starting right now.

_____ **CASE 13** _____
The Next Hours: How to Handle the Blow

"When I lost my job, I drove around for hours because I was so hurt and angry about the whole experience," remembers Tanya, a research assistant at an insurance firm. "They had called the whole company, several hundred of us, into the auditorium and given us assigned seats, then gave us the news and said, 'There's no fair way to do this, so those of you who are leaving will find a red sticker under your chair.' I couldn't believe how cold the company was about the process, and I knew if I was around anyone, I'd go to pieces. I needed time to myself to work it out in my head before I faced my husband or any of my friends."

Hector, a writer for a daily newspaper, went straight to a bar, but then decided it was the wrong thing to do. "I knew as soon as I sat down that I'd just drink until I made a fool of myself, and that it wouldn't do any good anyway. So I left and went to this quiet park and sat on the bench for a while until I calmed down. I just didn't have the guts to go home until I had something positive to tell my family, until I had some hope about how our future would turn out OK."

Says Joan, a marketing manager, "When I found out my position had been terminated, I was shocked. I had been at the company only a month, and I had left a great job on the other side of the country to take it. I just went home and sat in the dark, thinking, 'What am I going to do?' After a while, a few answers started popping into my head, and I realized the situation wasn't really that bad."

"When I lost my job, I actually went out and celebrated," laughs Peter, a construction worker. "We all knew the company was in bad shape, so we were just waiting for the final announcement. I didn't have the motivation to jump ship like a lot of others, so when it happened, it was the biggest relief you could imagine."

6

How Could This Happen To Me?!
Sorting Out Your Emotions— Safely

To say you're upset is an understatement. And to say you're devastated only uncovers the tip of your emotions.

What are the stages you are going through, and what can you expect later in the weeks to come? Most commonly, say psychologists and counselors, as well as former employees, you'll have the following symptoms, and the suggestions that follow have helped others move through them with strength and success.

1. **Disbelief or denial.** Not me, you're thinking. How could this happen to me? I'm a good worker. I gave years of commitment to that company. I spent my time and my energy for them. They can't just take away my job! I must be dreaming. I'll go in Monday and they'll beg me to come back. Or, they'll call me tomorrow. Not me. I couldn't have lost my job.

This stage usually doesn't last very long, perhaps only until the first day you got up and realize you really don't have a job to go back to. Your denial is your protection against the pain of your emotions, so you must get over your shock and accept the fact that you have been laid off or fired, and understand the reasons why. Only then can you begin to feel the emotions, and work through them to become a better, stronger person who can work towards a better life.

2. **The emotions.** First, you're going to feel angry and betrayed. How could the company to which you were so loyal take away something that was so important to you? That anger may run very deep, and to

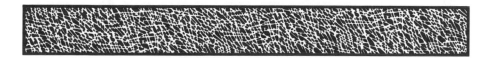

diffuse it you must be able to forgive the company and relieve yourself of the blame. Realize that:

- The company did what it had to do, because, ultimately, the survival of the company, in their eyes, is more important than the survival of the individual employee.

- It wasn't your choice to lose your job, but now that you have, the rest of your life can be made up of actions that *you* decide.

Then, you're going to feel sad, even depressed, for the loss of a job is typical of the grief felt with any death. And right now the bottom line is that your unemployment means a loss of concrete proof of your intelligence, skills, and capabilities. You'll also feel a loss of confidence. Your company doesn't believe in you any more, so who will? To fight these feelings, think about other activities in which you participate that utilize your mind and your skills. For examples, have a look at chart 6.1.

Next comes embarrassment, the humiliation of losing something so valuable you took for granted, and the shame of thinking about how in the world you are going to tell anyone else about it. For suggestions on approaching that situation, see chapter 7 and remember, losing your job was something you couldn't control because it probably wasn't your choice, it was the company's. But now you have the freedom to choose what you desire, and there's no shame in that whatsoever.

After going through these emotions, you may even feel relieved. Perhaps you knew the cutbacks were coming, and now that burden of worry is off your mind. Or you might have hated your job and the ax was the best thing that could have happened. Many employees state that when they were actually told they were being laid off or fired, a great weight slipped from their consciences because they finally knew what was going to happen and had a direction in which to start moving again in their lives. Some employees are actually happy after a long, or perhaps boring, career with little change in responsibility, few challenges, low pay, coworker conflict, management misunderstandings, or just plain bad business, and they feel good about the opportunity to get out of their ruts because it's a leap they couldn't have made under any other circumstances.

3. **Confusion and stress.** When you have thought about your feelings and worked through the reasons behind your emotions, you may feel empty and confused, as if you don't know what to do or where to go. That's OK. You probably don't. All that is burning into your mind at this point is worry—bills, family, health, getting a new job . . . what are you going to do?

Make a list, immediately. If you filled out the budget and contact worksheets in chapter 3, great; if not, go back and do them now. What are your debts? Your assets? What are your job prospects? Who can help you out? After your chapter 3 worksheets, fill out chart 6.2 by listing everything that is on your mind. Then, take a break. On Monday morning, you'll have a full schedule of important things to do.

CHART 6.1

Yes, You Still Have Many Skills

We know that even though you have lost your job, you haven't lost your talent or your determination. Now prove it to yourself!

Intelligence

_____

_____

_____

Communication

_____

_____

_____

Organization

_____

_____

_____

List another skill

_____

_____

_____

Creativity

_____

_____

_____

Leadership

_____

_____

_____

Determination

_____

_____

_____

And another

_____

_____

_____

CHART 6.2

What Is Worrying You, and How Can You Ease Your Anxiety?

List your biggest worries right now:

Example: I'll have to cut back on my expenses.

Example: I need a new job.

NOW, YOU TRY IT!

Your biggest worries:

_____

_____

_____

_____

_____

_____

_____

_____

_____

What action can you take to relieve this worry?

Figure out what I owe, then plan a weekly budget and stick to it.

Call contacts to see if they might have leads.
Look in the paper and trade journals for jobs.
Think about all my options to see if I really want the same position and field.

Your best actions:

_____

_____

_____

_____

_____

_____

_____

_____

_____

It's scary. You feel as if you're on the edge of a sharp precipice, standing backwards in a strong wind that might push you over into a bottomless pit of darkness. But keeping busy will help you cope with your anxiety and give you the confidence you need to survive and carry on—successfully—long after the loss of your job. Guided by your priorities and commitments, you also will have a better picture of where your life stands right now, as well as new directions in which you can turn.

And, when your lists are finished and you're aware of the things you need to do, you'll worry a lot less and sleep much better.

4. **Acceptance and determination.** Now that you know what your job meant to you, how much your feelings can influence your thoughts, and what you need to do, get going! You have lost your job, but now you realize that in the long run, it wasn't the only thing that meant something to you, nor has the experience taken any of your skills away. You still have your intelligence, your talent, your dreams, and your ambition, and these characteristics will always stay with you, no matter which direction you decide to take for your life.

Now what you need is the confidence in your abilities and belief in yourself that you will turn your life around for the better. Taking care of everything on your "to do" list (chart 6.3) will start giving you that confidence and belief in yourself. Remember:

You are the person you believe you are.
So believe in yourself, your intelligence, and your capabilities.
And then use them.

COUNSELING

Obviously, you're not going to be able to work through this type of devastating experience in a day, nor will you be able to do it alone. After taking some time—an hour, a day, a weekend—to think about your feelings and your future, it may help to talk with someone you trust who will listen and understand: a spouse, a friend, a family member, a coworker. Just having someone who will express confidence in your abilities and your future will add greatly to your peace of mind.

Not everyone has someone to help them out, however, and not everyone can handle the experience in just one try. Many larger companies provide outplacement services that offer counseling, as mentioned in chapter 4, or they can recommend good counseling firms. If not, professional help can be expensive, even if you feel you only need one session to sort out your feelings and goals.

There are low-cost and free options available, though; check out chart 6.4 for ideas. And don't be afraid to call. You feel terrible, but you're not the first person to reach out for help in a tough situation. It's your life now, and if you need help, you have to take the first step to get it. Even if you're not sure what you want or need to talk about, just call.

CHART 6.3

Now, for Your Plan of Action: The 'To Do' List!

Take all of your best actions from the previous chart and prioritize them on this page. Now you have a list of things to do first thing in the morning, or Monday morning, depending on when you're filling this out. And keep writing down your worries as the days pass by, along with your best actions to relieve them. This way, you'll have a great game plan that will ultimately lead you to success!

Priority actions (in order):

1. _____

2. _____

3. _____

4. _____

5. _____

6. _____

7. _____

8. _____

9. _____

10. _____

CHART 6.4

Low-Cost Counseling Options

Here are a few places to look for free or low-cost counseling if you need it. Many will be willing to give you a sliding fee.

- Hospitals

- Clinics

- Organizations

- Men's and women's groups

- Churches

- Colleges and universities

- National referral services

- Company referral services

- Employment bureau recommendations

- Yellow Pages

CASE 14
Emotional Expectations

"It's tough to give people hope," remarks Andrea, a counselor at a large outplacement firm. "When they lose their jobs, it's like any other life loss, such as the death of a spouse or parent, a divorce, or a terminal illness. I find that the process of going through recovery from it is like putting a magnifying glass on your life, and those who are already going through other issues at the time don't have the enthusiasm and self-esteem to bounce back as quickly. The introverted usually have more trouble than the extroverted, as well. It's the people who have the internal ability to deal with the world, the people with a sense of humor and flexibility, who are more easily able to become enthusiastic and proceed with their lives."

She adds that an important factor in recovering from the loss of a job is the individual's "locus of control," or whether the person feels that their life is controlled by him- or herself, or by the hands of fate. "Those who feel that they control their own lives, that the changes within them are things they personally can control instead of their being due to external factors around them, are more able to handle the changes. Those who feel fate is in control need to become more tuned in to the reality of the working world and see that these changes are occurring all over. They need to take their job loss beyond the personalized point of view and become more optimistic about the future. After all, you can either suck lemons or you can make lemonade."

_____ CASE 15 _____
Staying Motivated

"The main thing you need to do to stay motivated after the loss of your job, the main thing I tell those I counsel, is to first believe in yourself and your capabilities," advises Doug, an outplacement counselor for a national firm. "If you don't have confidence in yourself, it's hard to believe you can do anything, and it's hard to make anyone else believe in your capabilities either. You need to think back on the things you have done in your life, from the smallest accomplishments to the things of which you're most proud, and remember the feelings you had at the time."

Many psychologists and counselors agree that the loss of a job can be a devastating experience, one that often hits so quickly and with such force that it is hard for the employee to move in any direction at all, much less bounce back with enthusiasm. "I've seen people become very angry, and I've seen people break down and cry," Doug continues, "because it was so hard for them to accept the fact that they had lost their job. They felt like a failure and they thought that is the way they would be for the rest of their lives. So we work through the emotions and then focus on what they *have* done, which accomplishments they know they have achieved in the past, no matter how small or unimportant they may seem. Then, when they grasp some of that confidence again, we can focus on their goals for the future and what they need to do, and *can* do, to reach them."

7

Truth or Consequence?
What to Tell Your Family, Friends, and Future Employers

Even after you have accepted the fact yourself, one of the toughest parts about losing your job, whether by layoff or termination, is admitting it to others.

Why? Because most people equate their jobs with success. A job means security, and income, and it gives you a title that tells others what you can do. Broken down, this means that you may feel now, since you no longer have a title or company, that you can no longer do anything at all, and no one else will believe in your abilities.

Wrong! If you were laid off, it was through no fault of your own, and, in any case, your unemployment is only temporary. Soon you will find a good position in a good company on your own. And, if you show that you believe it, others will feel confident about your future as well. Even if you were fired or had to resign, don't worry. It has happened to many people who have gone on to new companies and now careers that turned out to be even more successful and satisfying. You may recognize a few of the names; see chart 7.1 for some good examples.

So, stand up and take a deep breath and tell people confidently that you were laid off, or that your position was terminated, and say it *without* apology, guilt, or embarrassment. It happened, but what's done is done; you can't dwell on it or let it hold you back from meeting people, going places, and trying for new jobs. You have to move forward, so show others that you accept the fact and you're doing something about

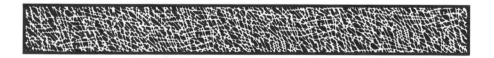

CHART 7.1

Some Famous People Who Lost Their Jobs

- Author Rudyard Kipling was fired from his job as a reporter at *The San Francisco Examiner*. His pink slip said, in essence, that he did not know how to use the English language. At the time he was fired, however, he had already written *The Man Who Would Be King* and went on to write other beloved classics such as *Kim* and *The Jungle Book*.

- Actress Raquel Welch was fired from the film *Cannery Row* only a few days after filming began.

- Actress Sean Young was replaced in her role as reporter Vicki Vale in the film *Batman* by Kim Basinger.

- Former NBC president Fred Silverman lost his million-dollar job, but went on to produce films.

- Ballet dancer Gelsey Kirkland lost her job with the American Ballet Theater for not showing up at rehearsals.

- Journalist Sally Quinn documents her troubled times in television in her book, *We're Going to Make You a Star*. Her later books, the novels *Regrets Only* and its sequel, *Happy Endings*, have gone on to become best-sellers.

- And then there was the NBC morning news battle between Jane Pauley, Deborah Norville, and Faith Daniels. But they weren't the only ones; Ruth Batchelor was once fired as ABC's gossip reporter on "Good Morning America."

- Politics make strange bedfellows, especially when the names John Sununu, Mikhail Gorbachev, and, yes, Richard Nixon are involved.

it. It will make it much easier for them to understand and accept the fact as well.

YOUR FAMILY

Your family will probably be the first to hear the news, and they will know by your face when you walk through the door, so there's no use in hiding the fact from them. And you're a team, bonded by blood and common dreams and loyalty, remember? Most likely, your family will want to help you through this time in your life with kindness, encouragement, and understanding.

They know you feel responsible for them; you may be the sole breadwinner in your home, or your income is what makes the car or house payments and keeps the kids in school. They know that you feel guilty about losing that security, that you feel ashamed that you couldn't have somehow held onto your job, and that your emotions will be on edge for a while.

And your family knows that you're feeling all of these things because you love them, and because you don't want to let them down and disappoint their hopes, but now you feel you have. They understand, so don't be afraid to tell your family, your wife or husband, your parents or your siblings. Don't be afraid to ask for their help and encouragement, either. The more people you have keeping their eyes out for job contacts and openings, the better.

Your family also can help you plan financial and educational changes, if necessary, so the sooner they know about the situation, the sooner you can work together to find successful suggestions. And the more people who stand behind your abilities, the more confidence you'll show to future job prospects and the quicker you'll find that new job. You'll have the constant enthusiasm and energy to stay motivated and keep looking until you find what you desire.

YOUR FRIENDS

If your friends truly are friends, you shouldn't have a problem telling them about your job situation. In fact, for a lot of people, it's easier to admit the fact to a close friend than anyone else, not only because that person isn't immediately affected by the crisis as a family is, but also because he or she can provide an empathetic ear and commonsense suggestions based on experience, rather than emotion. Many of your friends might be in the same field or career level as you, and if they know you're available for hire, they can spread the word quickly, along with a good recommendation.

CHART 7.2

How to Break the News

1. **Get to the point.** Tell your family or friends about the situation in a clear, concise manner. The longer you hide or drag out the news, the harder it will be for everyone. And, the sooner you say it, the sooner you'll be able to come up with solutions to moving on with your life.

2. **Provide alternatives.** You may have lost your job, but you will get another one, so give your listeners the details of your game plan. What will your first step be? Where will you look for employment? How soon will you start? What are other things you will need to do? As soon as you show your family and friends that it isn't going to get you down or cause you to sit on your rear sulking, they'll respect your determination and drive. Then they can help you fine-tune your game plan with suggestions and advice.

3. **Cover your financial bases.** If money is going to be tight, get it out on the table with your family right away. Work out a plan that cuts back on spending, and include your children in the discussion. It is a situation that the whole family needs to handle together, and they may be able to offer ideas from a different point of view. Also, being treated as adults in a very adult situation will give them a realistic glimpse of the working world and teach them valuable lessons they might have to use themselves someday.

4. **Deal with hostility, anger, and doubt.** There will be a lot of emotions during the discussion, so take the time to explore the reasons behind them. Your husband or wife may fear taking on the monetary burden for an uncertain amount of time, your children may think losing a job means losing a home and starving, your friends may be angry because they think of job loss as failure. Whatever the feelings, it is important to know who is having them and why; then you can diffuse them and work together toward viable solutions to the situation.

5. **Try to stay calm, and to stay until the end.** If emotions arise, take a deep breath and continue. Don't walk out. Running away only prolongs the hostility and fear. Make sure you have enough time, and express your feelings as well as you can.

YOUR FUTURE JOB PROSPECTS

Honesty is the best policy. Isn't it? In an interview situation, or on a job application, it can become a bit tricky, especially if you were fired for a touchy reason. So, what do the experts recommend?

First, here is some advice from employers around the country on how they feel if they find out an applicant has been laid off or fired:

- References, as well as previous job listings, are always checked for accuracy. So be honest, because the company doing the background check is going to find out anyway.

- Just because you were laid off or fired doesn't mean a company won't hire you. In fact, many employees in high-turnover fields know that layoffs and firings and job changes are just part of life in their occupation.

- Be honest. If you were laid off, the hiring company will most likely understand. If you resigned or were fired, you don't have to go into great detail about the circumstances. That was in the past. Show the company the kind of commitment and good work you will be doing for them, and then back up your words with solid examples.

- A lot of people have lost jobs in their lifetimes. But they have found new and even better work afterwards. Don't let your low self-esteem keep you from applying. If your work is good and your morale is high, there will always be a job somewhere for you.

IF YOU JUST CAN'T DO IT

Sometimes, however, your emotions will affect you more deeply and for a longer time than you first realized, and even after several weeks, or months, it's hard to tell people that you lost your job. You could be in a profession that traditionally looks down on those who have been through the experience. Or you could have unsympathetic relatives, or simply a case of low self-esteem.

Without lying, there are a few handy phrases that wax over the depth of the matter and help you save face until you—and others—are ready to accept the situation head-on:

- I've temporarily lost my job due to the economy

- I'm taking some time off to explore my options

- I've resigned to look for a more challenging position

- I'm pursuing freelance work

- I've decided to look for a company that will appreciate the skills I have to offer

- I decided my skills would be more useful in another position (or field)

- There was nowhere for me to move up and excel within the company, so I realized it was time to move on

- I wasn't using my skills to the best of my ability

- I wasn't challenged

- I am looking for a more satisfying and rewarding career.

These are just a few ideas used by employees who have been laid off or fired. But remember, humans by nature are generous, understanding, and willing to help one another. You're down, so be honest and ask for help, and show your true goals and ambitions, along with your excitement to achieve them. It will demonstrate your understanding and acceptance of the past, as well as your enthusiasm about getting on with the future, making your family, friends, and employment prospects far more receptive to and respectful of your situation.

_____ CASE 16 _____
Breaking the News to Others

"I was too embarrassed to tell anyone right away that I lost my job," admits Melissa, a retail store manager. "It wasn't as if the conditions were questionable. The company was simply cutting back on staff. But I was ashamed that it was *me* who had to leave; why not some of the others who hadn't been there as long, or who seemed less valuable? I don't know, I sort of shirked the issue for a few weeks by telling people I quit to look for a better position until I could face the facts about what happened and accept the situation myself."

"I've always been honest with my family," says Alex, a factory supervisor, "so I had no trouble telling them what had happened. They were wonderful . . . they realized how scared I was and how much it hurt, and they really pulled together to make me feel good, like I was worth something. That was what gave me the confidence to keep going."

"It took me a while to admit that I'd been fired," remarks Monica, who worked at a machine repair company. "I mean, I told my husband because I had to, but I avoided telling my friends and my parents until I had a few good job prospects, and I had my head together. Before that, I was way too depressed to even talk about it. I would have started to cry."

"It was terrible to admit it to anyone at first, but once I did, I found that people really understood," remembers Zachary, a public relations assistant. "Not only that, but they really wanted to help. That's how I found the job I have today—because someone believed in me and recommended me for it."

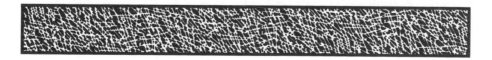

8

Money Matters:
Budgeting, Bargaining, and Braving the Unemployment Office

Once you get past your emotions and the fear of telling others about your job loss, your first worry will probably be about money.

The paychecks may have stopped coming, but that doesn't mean the bills or the little expenditures or the yearly fees or the emergencies will end. If you haven't already, fill out chart 3.7 to give you an overall grasp of your finances. Then, fill out chart 8.1 with your totals, and write down a few immediate suggestions on how you can cut back on your expenses.

Now you can compare what you have with what you owe, and what you're going to have to pay each month just to keep the debt collectors off your back. And, you can examine the options you have for your assets: the house, the car, the furniture, the boat, the motorcycle, and so on. If your debts are high, chart 8.2 offers a few suggestions on how to cut back and make ends meet without too much pain.

If you're particularly ambitious, there are many ways you can make money on the side while looking for a new job, especially if you have good connections in several different fields. Are you the member of a professional club or association? Which skills do you use off the job? What are your hobbies? Chart 8.3 gives you various suggestions that have been used by others who lost their jobs to bring in a little extra money during the time they were out of work. Some were actually so successful at one or more of these ideas that they never did return to

CHART 8.1

Do You Know What You Owe?

Take your asset, debt, and bill totals from chart 3.7 and fill them in here.

$_____ assets

$_____ debts

$_____ monthly bills

Now the figures are clear, where you can find them at any time. While you're at it, though, write down some ways in which you could cut back on your monthly spending:

1. _____

2. _____

3. _____

4. _____

5. _____

6. _____

7. _____

8. _____

their original field; they simply stuck to running their own business for good, and enjoyed it thoroughly.

Sometimes, however, the bills are just too much. When you don't have a job, many companies are willing to lower or delay debts until you can afford to pay them again—as long as you *do* pay them—if you inform them of your situation. Write a letter to those you owe money and explain your situation and your commitment to paying them as

CHART 8.2

Making Ends Meet

When you're worrying about your finances and your severance and vacation pay don't amount to much, your savings may not get you very far. What do the experts recommend doing to cut your costs?

Cut off all unnecessary bills immediately. Some areas that can be pared down include:

Entertainment. Cable TV, movies, video rentals, nightlife entertainments, parties, and so on.

Travel. Take your vacation close to home, if not at home. Or, go to a friend's or relative's home.

Food. Don't eat out. Make out a weekly menu and grocery list and stick to it. Pack lunches and cut out tobacco and alcoholic beverages.

Shopping. Stop spending on your credit cards. Don't spend money on anything that you don't absolutely need.

Impulse buys. Cut down on soda, gum, candy, and trinkets. Every dollar adds up, especially now.

Clubs. Fees and dues for meetings, memberships, events, and lunches can take a big bite out of your savings. If the contacts aren't necessary, don't sign up again. Also, exercise at home.

Publications. Newspaper and magazine subscriptions take a toll on your wallet. You can read them for free at the library.

Transportation. Cut down on driving to save gas and money. Take public transportation or get a ride from a friend, family member, or local car pool.

Utilities. Cut down your bills by conserving water, electricity, gas, and making fewer long-distance phone calls.

- **Sell what you can.**
  Furniture, cars, jewelry, clothes, artwork, and so on are all included here. If you need cash fast and you don't need the possessions, this is a good way to get money quickly.

continued

- **Consolidate your expenses.**
  If you're starting to sink into debt, there are probably credit counseling services in your area that would be glad to help you. Warning: Check to see if a fee or monthly percentage is involved; it could turn out to be more than you can afford in the long run.

- **Move.**
  This applies mainly to apartment-dwellers. If your rent is high, you can cut it down by moving out. And you'll get your deposit back if you need cash. Consider doubling up with one or more roommates.

- **Explain your situation.**
  Write a letter to each of your creditors telling them that you have lost your job, but you have every intention of paying them as soon as you have a steady income. Most companies will be willing to work with you.

- **Save your receipts.**
  Some of your job-search expenses can be written off on your tax form. Call the IRS for details and to see if this rule still is allowed.

---

soon as you can. Follow up with a call to reiterate your intentions and put a friendly voice to your promise. If you owe them money, you can bet your collectors will get back with you again soon, and usually they'll try to be as flexible as possible, because a little money on a regular basis is far better than no money at all.

UNDERSTANDING UNEMPLOYMENT

You have probably seen the television ads for buying American products, the ones where they show the long, sad faces of those in the unemployment line. Perhaps you have heard the slow, depressing descriptions that are lyricized in a few well-known songs. In many ways, these images are very real; filing for unemployment benefits isn't fun, it isn't a happy place, and there aren't a lot of hopeful smiles.

But it's a place you need to confront, because your company pays into a fund, and that fund is there to help you out—now. It doesn't cost you anything except the time spent in their offices; nothing came out of your paycheck for unemployment benefits while you were still working for your company. Claiming your unemployment benefits will give you up to half of the salary of your previous position, up to a certain amount,

CHART 8.3

Making Money on the Side

- **Write articles** on your areas of expertise for local papers, magazines, and trade journals. Give the editor a call, or pick up the *Writer's Market* in your library reference section for details.

- **Talk about what you know.** Sign up with a local speaker's bureau or a local or national organization directory for speakers. Local talk shows, both TV and radio, might have an interest in your topics and ideas, though they don't always pay their guests.

- **Make your hobby pay.** Do you paint? Write? Play music? Make crafts? Work in a home shop? Fix cars? Ask around your community and the city to see if you can drum up some interest in a business. If you need help on how to get started, try your local library business section.

- **Computer tactics.** If you have a computer at home, you can write resumes and cover letters, design flyers, and type reports and papers. Check out local colleges and businesses for interest in these services.

- **Teach what you know.** Some community centers and businesses might be interested in holding a seminar that involves your expertise. Or, you can set up a class or a lecture for a small fee.

---

depending on the state in which you were employed. And, for a lot of displaced workers who need a boost to get back on their feet and into the work force, that's reason enough to go.

Here's how it works: If you're an employee who has been laid off or fired, you should get to the unemployment office (possibly listed under "Employment Bureau" in your phone book) as soon as you can after losing your job. There, you'll fill out a few forms and then return for an orientation meeting, in which you may either see a video or attend a class that explains the claim qualification and filing process.

You'll also learn how much compensation you're entitled to, for how long, and what to do if you find part- or full-time work while still using the system. Your unemployment office will have some type of job reference system, where prospective employers come in and check out applications, conduct on-the-spot interviews, and provide employees with information on future openings. You may also be assigned to a job counselor, who will help you choose an occupational category and discuss with you where and with whom some of your best prospects might be.

In addition, you will receive an unemployment booklet to help you keep track of your checks, to remind you of all the guidelines of the system, and to record your progress in your job search. Yes, you do have to be actively looking for work, and be able to document your efforts, to receive unemployment funds. But look at it this way: It's money that will help you get your bills paid and put food on the table during your job search. There's nothing to be embarrassed or feel guilty about when you use the system to claim the funds. In the offices, you'll find people of all ages and career backgrounds, in three-piece suits and jeans, who are using the system to help them. And that's the whole purpose of unemployment, to help *you*. So don't refuse the offer because you think it will hurt your image or because you feel you don't need it. You do.

The unemployment claimants and officers also have a few comments and suggestions for you:

- Unemployment isn't for the poor or the lazy. It's for anyone who needs help supporting themselves and their family; anyone who needs help getting things together when they've lost their job. Anyone.

- If you go into the unemployment office with the attitude that you're going to do something with your life, that this isn't the end of it, and you're not too good for it, you're going to get out of there that much faster. And you're going to influence a lot of other people around you by making them feel they won't be out of work forever, either.

- The unemployment people are on your side. They see thousands of people like you every day; angry, depressed, desperate. They understand.

- The wait could be long, so get there early and bring something to read or something to do. But talk to other people and share your experiences. You'll find your situation isn't that bad if you listen to the people around you. And you'll meet some pretty interesting characters and make a bond with others who feel as crummy as you do.

- Be upfront with your unemployment counselor. If you're having trouble legally, emotionally, or professionally, let them know. Your counselor can suggest ways to help, and to get help. After all, they're the experts, and they've pushed thousands of people back to success in their careers and their lives.

When you have your financial situation under control, with your bills and expenses and cutbacks figured out, use chart 8.4 to document your weekly expenditures. At this stage, it is very important to keep track of where every penny of your savings is going so you can use your money wisely. Make several blank copies of the chart to use in the weeks to come, and keep it where you can find it easily.

CHART 8.4

Your Financial Schedule

Month _____

Week 1		**Week 2**		**Week 3**		**Week 4**	
Expenses:		Expenses:		Expenses:		Expenses:	
_____	$_____	_____	$_____	_____	$_____	_____	$_____
_____	$_____	_____	$_____	_____	$_____	_____	$_____
_____	$_____	_____	$_____	_____	$_____	_____	$_____
_____	$_____	_____	$_____	_____	$_____	_____	$_____
_____	$_____	_____	$_____	_____	$_____	_____	$_____
_____	$_____	_____	$_____	_____	$_____	_____	$_____
_____	$_____	_____	$_____	_____	$_____	_____	$_____
_____	$_____	_____	$_____	_____	$_____	_____	$_____
Total	$_____	Total	$_____	Total	$_____	Total	$_____
Income:		Income:		Income:		Income:	
_____	$_____	_____	$_____	_____	$_____	_____	$_____
_____	$_____	_____	$_____	_____	$_____	_____	$_____
_____	$_____	_____	$_____	_____	$_____	_____	$_____
_____	$_____	_____	$_____	_____	$_____	_____	$_____
Total	$_____	Total	$_____	Total	$_____	Total	$_____
End Total +/−		End Total +/−		End Total +/−		End Total +/−	
	$_____		$_____		$_____		$_____

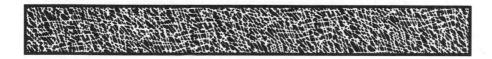

9

Scheduling Your Life:
How to Open Your Mind to Your Freedom

Think about your life for a moment. What have you done with it from birth until now? What have you accomplished? Education? A family? Wealth? Independence? And now, where do you want to go?

Your job loss has actually given you two things you wouldn't otherwise have: the gifts of freedom and time. Not many people get the chance to really examine their lives and skills, to really think about and explore what makes them happy and then choose the best career to suit them. Would you have used your vacation to do it? No, there wouldn't be nearly enough time. Would you have taken a leave of absence to think and explore, or would you have quit your job altogether? It's doubtful, but now you have that freedom to figure out what you really would like to do with your life.

So get excited, because that's where you're headed next!

BUILD YOUR CONFIDENCE

Although you have accepted your job loss and worked through your feelings, you may still lack the belief in your talents and goals that you'll need to open your mind. If you haven't done so, sit down alone or with your family, a counselor, or a few friends, and fill out chart 3.8 by list-

CHART 9.1

Which Skills Do You Consider Most Important to Use in Your Next Job?

1. _____

2. _____

3. _____

4. _____

5. _____

6. _____

7. _____

8. _____

9. _____

10. _____

11. _____

12. _____

ing your proven job skills, those you use in other activities and the skills you think you have, but don't get the chance to use. If you already completed this worksheet, turn back and try to add a few more ideas in each column. Then, fill out chart 9.1 with the skills that are most important to you, the ones you would definitely like to use in your next career.

Now, open your mind.

RULE 1: THERE ARE NO RULES

This is the fun part, where you get to *really* dream. Anything! Use chart 9.2 to write down things you dream of doing and being. Flying planes? Being a nurse or doctor? Running a scuba diving business? And it doesn't have to be all career related, either; if you really dream of having a family, traveling around the world, or learning to sing, write it down! In the end, it all will connect together.

Have fun!

STUDY YOUR FAULTS

You've been alive long enough to realize that you do have a few faults, no matter how small they might be. But there's nothing that says you can't change. So fill out chart 9.3 with any drawbacks you think might keep you from getting to your goals.

EXAMINE YOUR ENVIRONMENT

Remember your last look around the office? Now is the time to draw on that experience. What were your thoughts and impressions? Did you really like your surroundings? What did you like about the people with whom you worked? Which parts of your job did you enjoy the most? What would you have changed if you could?

Use chart 9.4 to list your work preferences, noting specifically what you didn't like and what you really enjoyed about your previous position. This will help you narrow down the outside job factors and focus on the specific things you're looking for within your new career.

ACCEPT YOUR ADVANTAGES

In addition to some faults and a few changes in your work environment, you have a lot of gifts in your personality and thoughts that will win over a prospective employer. Use chart 9.5 to write in these advantages—and don't be modest. These are some of the characteristics employers of every field look for in job candidates, and they can help you shine out above the competition. Place an "X" by the characteristics that especially helped you in the past, and an "*" by the advantages you haven't used but would like to try out in the future.

CHART 9.2

Dare to Dream!

What Are Your Ultimate Career Fantasies?

1. For which companies would you love to work? In which department or position?

Company: _____   Dept./Position: _____

_____   _____

_____   _____

_____   _____

_____   _____

2. Or, if you were in control of your own business, what would it be? Where, and what size? Local, national, or international? Who would you hire to work with you? Add your own details in a short paragraph.

_____

_____

_____

_____

_____

_____

3. Picture yourself in that ideal job: your feelings, procedures, clothing, office, etc.

_____

_____

_____

continued

4. How would you like other people to see you?

_____

_____

_____

_____

5. What other career goals or dreams do you have?

_____

_____

_____

_____

6. What other experiences and accomplishments would you like to add to your life?

_____

_____

_____

_____

CHART 9.3

Study Your Faults

List your possible faults here:

How can you change to avoid this problem in your next job?

Example: Trouble meeting deadlines, always procrastinating

Start projects when they are assigned, divide and prioritize daily, and follow schedule until job is finished on time.

1. _____

2. _____

3. _____

4. _____

5. _____

6. _____

7. _____

8. _____

CHART 9.4

Examine Your Environment

1. What did you really enjoy about your last job in each category?

environment	people	work itself
_____	_____	_____
_____	_____	_____
_____	_____	_____
_____	_____	_____

2. What would you have changed? Why?

environment	people	work itself
_____	_____	_____
_____	_____	_____
_____	_____	_____
_____	_____	_____

3. What else would you like to include for your next career?

environment	people	work itself
_____	_____	_____
_____	_____	_____
_____	_____	_____
_____	_____	_____

CHART 9.5

Accept Your Clear Advantages

From Chart 3.8, when you wrote down the skills you used on and off the job, choose those that you feel are your strongest, however many it may be. And don't be modest; if you have talent, you only live once, so use it!

List your strengths here:

1. _____

2. _____

3. _____

4. _____

5. _____

6. _____

7. _____

8. _____

9. _____

10. _____

11. _____

12. _____

13. _____

14. _____

Now, go back and mark those that helped you in the past, and those you would like to use in your next job.

X   helped you in the past   *   would like to use in future

LOOK OVER THE HORIZON

All you have before you now are possibilities, leads on your future and your satisfaction in life and your career. The choices . . . well, they're up to you to explore. Just remember:

> There are no rules that state you have to work in a certain profession or be a certain type of person.

So, keep your mind open to all of your opportunities.

Next, look at the list of careers in chart 9.6 and consider how your skills might align with the careers you think you would like to have at this point. Do any of them match? In the blanks write in your top choices in order, then check off what it will take for you to get started in that field. Money? Education? Experience? Time? Or do you have a diverse background and connections that can get your foot in the door? Use chart 9.7 to list the people from your original contact worksheet (chart 3.6) who could either help you get into the field or give you a good grasp on what you need to be successful in a particular job category—before you jump head-first into the opportunity.

A NOTE ON NETWORKING

It is one of the most important things you can do right now: talking with, getting advice from, and using the guidance of other professionals who are already established in the fields in which you are looking. Take your list of career prospects and the contacts who could give you information, and mark the top three in each category. Now, compose a letter expressing your interest in the field or in talking with them about suggestions or ideas about new openings. Refer to the examples in chart 9.8.

This isn't a request for a job; it's simply a request to talk about experiences and possibilities with someone who knows the field well. If your contact is a friend you can just get together or give him or her a call. In your letter include your phone number, and then follow up with a phone call in a week or so after you send the letter, explaining who you are and why you are interested in talking about their profession. Most executives are very receptive to helping others and will be excited to take fifteen minutes to an hour to give you a bit of insight on the career options.

Don't be shy, just be honest and enthusiastic, as well as professional. It's not an interview, but it is a professional meeting to indicate your interest, availability, and willingness to get out and learn. Treat it as an interview, though, in both dress and manner; you can even suggest bringing your resume and portfolio just for constructive criticism and suggestions. This gives your contact an idea of who you are and how good your work is, and he or she will be that much more likely to recommend your name to someone who has an opening.

CHART 9.6

Career Chart: Matching Your Skills

Are you looking to make a career move, or completely change your focus? Below are a few possibilities. Fill in the ones that appeal to you on the lines provided below. Then list the skills you have that will help you in that field. Finally, write down other actions you will need to take to succeed, such as getting a specific degree or license, learning more about opportunities, having specific references, adding to your background, and so on. Or, are you already prepared to enter the field? Complete the chart and see!

accounting
acting
advertising
aerospace
agriculture
airlines
animal care
appraisal/evaluation
architecture
automotive

banking
beauty culture
biological sciences
biotechnology
book publishing
broadcasting
building/construction
business communication
business management

cable television
carpentry
chemical engineering
chemistry
childcare
chiropractic care
civil engineering
commercial art
computer/graphic design
computer maintenance
computer science
counseling
crafts
culinary careers

dance
data processing
dental care
drafting

electrical trades
electronic/electrical engineering
energy careers
engineering technology
environmental concerns
eye care

fashion
fast food
federal government
film
finance
fire protection
fitness
food services
foreign languages
forestry

gerontology
government services
graphic communications

health and medicine
high-tech careers
home economics
hospital administration
hotel management
human resources

industrial design
insurance
interior design

journalism

landscape architecture
laser technology
law, law enforcement
library/information

machine trades
marketing
mechanical engineering
military careers
modeling
music careers

nursing
nutrition

occupational therapy

part-time work
performing arts
petroleum
pharmacy careers
photography
plumbing and pipe fitting
psychology

real estate
recreation and leisure
religious service

social science
social work careers
sports medicine

teaching
transportation/travel

vocational/technical careers

continued

Write down the fields or positions in which you are interested. Then, below them, list the skills you have that could help you succeed.

Example: Business management

Leadership skills, solid work experience, organized, good communication and negotiating skills, enjoy responsibility and supervision, work well with others, like to research and try new ideas

Now, what else will it take for you to start out or continue in this field?

Example:

Finish college degree
Talk with other managers to find different tactics
Bring proof of skills to interviews

1. _____   _____

2. _____   _____

3. _____   _____

4. _____   _____

continued

5. _____   _____

6. _____   _____

7. _____   _____

GREAT LEAPS OF FAITH

Sometimes, for workers who have lost their jobs, finding another one isn't enough. Instead, they take the time to travel, go back to school, freelance in their profession, and even start their own business.

These options not only take courage; they take careful planning, good sales skills, loyal clients, and substantial investments in both time and money. If one of these options, or something outside of the traditional work venue, attracts your fancy, talk to several people first: banks (loans), lawyers (laws of business and zoning), and accountants (financing your dream). You'll also need to do some careful research. Is the timing right for education? Is there a real purpose to traveling? Is there really a market for your freelance work or the business you're thinking of starting? Many community centers, companies, and colleges offer free business seminars. Check your phone book for sources, or your local library, bulletin boards, and trade journals for information.

Just for fun, chart 9.9 lists a few people who lost their jobs for one reason or another and then, through a leap of faith, found success in a completely different area. And there are plenty of excellent books to help you make career and life choices. Look in the business and psychology sections of your bookstore or library. A few to browse through might include:

CHART 9.7

Connecting Your Contacts

Career field and position possibilities: Who could help:

1. Field _____   _____

   Position _____   _____

2. Field _____   _____

   Position _____   _____

3. Field _____   _____

   Position _____   _____

4. Field _____   _____

   Position _____   _____

5. Field _____   _____

   Position _____   _____

CHART 9.8

Sample Contact or Networking Letter

Your name
Address
City, State, Zip

Date

Contact name
Title
Company
Address
City, State, Zip

Dear (contact name):

Currently, I am looking for information on and opportunities in the (field in which you're interested) profession, and I hope that you can provide me with a few good insights and suggestions.

This is not a request for a job opening, but rather a way to build a clear picture of avenues and opportunities within the (profession). I am talking with many people from all angles of this field, and every piece of information and suggestion is very valuable to me.

I would like to set up a time to meet with you for half an hour or so, at your convenience, to talk about these matters. I will call you on (day and date) to arrange a meeting.

Thank you for your time, and I welcome any suggestions or further information you will be able to bring to this meeting about this profession.

Sincerely,

(typed name here, with signature above it)

Sample Contact Letter for Networking

Your name
Address
City, State, Zip

Date

Contact name
Title
Company
Address
City, State, Zip

Dear (contact name):

I have observed with pleasure your success in the field of (example: account-ing), and due to your experience, I would like to talk with you about certain aspects of this profession.

Currently, I am seeking a position in (the field) and I would like to know more about the various career directions and requirements, as well as talk with you about the qualities and experiences that have helped you succeed.

I do not expect you to have or be able to recommend any current job open-ings. However, I would appreciate it if we could set up a time to discuss your suggestions and comments on your profession and how I could use my expe-rience and qualifications to succeed as well.

I realize your time is valuable, so I would like to schedule a brief meeting at your convenience. I will call you on (day and the date) to arrange a meeting.

Thank you for your time, and I look forward to speaking with you soon.

Sincerely,

(Your name typed here, with signature above it)

Sample Contact Letter from a Referral

Often, the people you contact to discuss the field, experiences, various positions, and so on will refer you to some of their associates who might be able to provide you with additional information. To schedule an appointment with contacts you don't know personally, you can use the same body of your original letter, with changes to the first paragraph.

Example: Dear Mr. Thomas:

Ms. Carolyn Jones, director of *XYZ, Inc.,* spoke highly of your experience and success in the (accounting) field and recommended that I discuss with you certain aspects of your profession.

(Add the rest of the letter here, or make up your own letter of referral that suits your situation.)

After you have met with each contact, do not forget to write them a note to thank them for their time and information, just as you would for a job interview. It could say something like this:

Example: Dear Ms Jones:

Thank you again for the opportunity to meet with you last *Thursday, January 12.*

I enjoyed the discussion very much and your suggestions were greatly appreciated. As you suggested, I have contacted *Mr. Jeff Thomas* and we will be meeting very soon to talk about opportunities and experiences in the (accounting) field.

If there is any further information you think of that might add to your previous comments, I would be grateful to hear them. Please feel free to call me at your convenience, and I will keep you informed on my progress.

CHART 9.9

Leaps of Faith

- Artist Claude Monet quit his job after he won 100,000 francs in the French lottery to take a shot at the career he really wanted to have: painting.

- Charlotte Brontë was once told by a literary critic that literature was not a woman's business and she should stick to "proper duties." She went on to write the classic *Jane Eyre*, among other books.

- Arthur Conan Doyle, an ophthalmologist, was also the creator of Sherlock Holmes.

- Before Fidel Castro turned to politics and revolution, he was a film extra in several Hollywood movies.

- Charles Goodyear, the creator of vulcanized rubber, began his experiments with the substance from a jail cell where he was being held for not paying his debts.

- Who was once a trained sniper in Israel? None other than sex therapist Dr. Ruth Westheimer.

- No school, no success? Not necessarily. Charles Dickens, Thomas Edison, and Mark Twain never attended a grade in high school. (Note: Today's requirements for success are a little different, however. In our society, education *is* the key to successfully achieving your dreams!)

Awaken the Giant Within
(Anthony Robbins, Summit Books)

Do It! Let's Get Off Our Buts
(John-Roger and Peter McWilliams, Prelude Press)

Learned Optimism
(Martin E. P. Seligman, Ph.D., Alfred A. Knopf)

The Magic of Thinking Big
(David J. Schwartz, Ph.D., Simon & Schuster)

Picking Up the Pieces
(Barbara Hansen, Ph.D., Taylor Publishing Company)

The Road Less Traveled
(M. Scott Peck, M.D., Simon & Schuster)

The Sky's the Limit
(Dr. Wayne Dyer, Pocket Books)

Unconditional Life: Mastering the Forces That Shape Personal Reality
(Deepak Chopra, M.D., Bantam Books)

What Color is Your Parachute?
(Richard Nelson Bolles, Ten Speed Press)

What Smart People Do When Losing Their Jobs
(Kathleen A. Riehle, John Wiley & Sons)

10

Monday Morning:
Get Up and Hit the Ground Running

The alarm goes off and you sit up with a jolt. Rubbing your eyes, you start to get out of bed and head for the shower when it suddenly hits you . . . Why? I no longer have a job.

Get up and get going anyway. If you have your "To Do" list from chapter 6, begin it. Clear a place at the table or a desk to make calls and have a notepad and paper ready to take down ideas. Compose letters for your contacts, fix your resume, and schedule a time to go to a copying center or the post office for stamps. You have a lot to do, and there's no time like the present to get on it.

Sure, it would be nice to ignore your problems and sink back into bed, hiding beneath the depression of losing your job. Don't do it! Every day you hide is a day you waste, a day less closer to achieving what you want out of life.

Besides, acting like a failure will make you and the rest of the world believe you are one. You are not a failure. You have many skills and goals, and with a bit of ambition, you can put them to work in the career of your choosing.

SCHEDULING

The first thing you'll need to do is set your goals by following the example in chart 10.1, then using chart 10.2 to formulate your own schedule

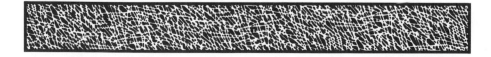

CHART 10.1

Sample Schedule for Success

Look at this example to see what you need to do to work towards your next career move. Then make copies of the following blank chart and fill out your own priorities and schedules:

Week: 1   Date: January 1

To do:

1. Visit unemployment office

2. Write contact letter

3. Choose contacts to network

4. Visit companies X, Y, and Z to apply

5. Send resume to ten jobs in Sunday paper

6. Schedule meeting with new insurance agent

7. Look at trade journals at library

8. Meet with director of speaker's bureau

9. Post office for stamps

10. Copy resume, cover letters

11. _____

12. _____

13. _____

14. _____

15. _____

16. _____

17. _____

18. _____

19. _____

20. _____

continued

	Monday	Tuesday	Wednesday	Thursday	Friday	Weekend
8:00	Unemp. office	Send resumes	Visit companies X,Y, and Z to apply	Unempl. meeting	Meet w/ contact	Call good contacts for leads
9:00						
		Library				
10:00						Decide if should
11:00	Contact temp. svc.			Drop resumes at employers downtown	Meet w/ career counselor	sell car
12:00						Discuss option of moving w/family
1:00	Write contact,	Write to companies found today in journals	Meet with contact			
2:00	cover letters				Write to ten more companies w/ openings	
3:00				Research at library		Clip Sun. job possib.
4:00	Copying center and post office	Call new insurance agent	Mail new letters to companies			Search bookstores for more references
5:00				Meet with new insurance agent		

of success. Not only will you have a guide to get you going and give you a purpose to start each day, but you also will have solid proof that you are accomplishing a lot during your off time. Some things suggested by previously unemployed workers to put in your schedule include:

- Contacting the unemployment office.

- Write your contact letters and mail them.

- Call the contacts you know and set up appointments.

- Rewrite your cover letter if necessary.

- Set a goal number of job openings to apply for each week.

- List companies for which you would like to work and send a letter of qualification and interest to the person who would be hiring you (a department manager or director or president, not personnel).

- Take a day to go to the offices of large companies and look at their job opening books. Then apply and leave a resume.

CHART 10.2

Your Schedule for Success

Week: _____   Date: _____

To do:

1. _____   11. _____
2. _____   12. _____
3. _____   13. _____
4. _____   14. _____
5. _____   15. _____
6. _____   16. _____
7. _____   17. _____
8. _____   18. _____
9. _____   19. _____
10. _____   20. _____

	Monday	Tuesday	Wednesday	Thursday	Friday	Weekend
8:00						
9:00						
10:00						
11:00						
12:00						
1:00						
2:00						
3:00						
4:00						
5:00						

- Use your library. Look in industry publications for job openings and in directories for companies that are doing well that might have openings that fit your qualifications.

- At the library, you can brush up on career advice and new events and appointments in your fields of choice.

MORE POSITIVE ACTION

Now that you have the time and flexibility, why not do some of the things you keep putting off when you're burned out on job hunting for the day like exercising, or learning to cook, or spending more time with your children or spouse, going to classes or lunch talks by local personalities, reading, taking a course at a local school, or picking up a hobby. Look at chart 10.3 for suggestions. You're going to need to take breaks, because your energy level is low, as is your self-esteem and courage. Keeping fit, active, and learning new things will raise your enthusiasm and confidence, and give you the courage to ask for what you want when you're close to getting your next job.

KEEPING YOUR CONFIDENCE UP

To begin your day with a burst of energy and get the most out of it, here are a few tips to start you off:

- **Get up at your usual time, and dress nicely.** When you're dressed, you feel as if you have places to go and things to do. And you do! So get up and get dressed every morning.

- **Eat healthy.** Sounds obvious, doesn't it? But more counselors recommend the basics, because more people under stress—like you—lose their appetite and skip meals, or eat too much. Watch it.

- **Don't watch television.** TV can be a drug; once you start watching, it's hard to pull away, except during the ads, perhaps. Stay away from it during the day, at least. Remember, normally you would be working anyway.

- **Stay in touch with your friends.** Along with your family, your friends are your best confidence boosters. When you need a shoulder to lean on or a pat on the back, call friends. They'll keep your enthusiasm up and your fears down.

- **Keep a diary.** Sure, you have a "To Do" list and a daily schedule, but that doesn't talk about feelings or doubts or hopes. A journal is a good end-of-day therapy that lets you get out your emotions be-

CHART 10.3

Positive Actions

- **Exercise:**
  Even try something new, like skating, boating, swimming, tennis, bowling, pool, golf, weights . . . whatever you'd like to try. Now is the time!

- **Get outside:**
  Take long walks; run in a park; explore your neighborhood, city, and even your own backyard.

- **Be loved:**
  Now you have time, so enjoy more of it with those you love. It will bring you closer and give you much-needed security.

- **Learn something new:**
  Chess, cooking, riding a bike, another language. Sign up for a free class, if available.

- **Culture:**
  Museums, theater, symphony, and poetry readings await. many are free.

- **Dare to do it!**
  Do something that you always thought you would hate. You may find you like it, and you'll open your mind at the same time.

---

fore you go to sleep. When you get a job, you can either pitch the diary or use it to help someone else out in the future by showing them how you felt and what you did to succeed.

- **Take off some of the pressure.** Although you'd probably like to, you won't get a job the first week, and probably not the second or third, either, unless your connections and timing are miraculous. Remember your first job search? It took time, and this one may take even longer, so be patient and enjoy your freedom and flexibility.

- **Keep your goals in sight.** Getting a job isn't your first priority; it's getting a job that is right for *you* and will bring *you* satisfaction.

Make your choices carefully, and get second opinions before jumping hastily into a situation you may later regret.

- **Be good to yourself.** Nearly every person who loses a job spends a great deal of time beating him- or herself up about it. Don't. Instead, take each day one at a time, and congratulate yourself on the small goals you make. Then look back a week later, and you'll find you have come quite a long way.

_____ **CASE 17** _____
Future Job Focus

What is the best way to project confidence in those first interviews? How can you highlight your accomplishments that will be most important to the job opening? How can you maintain enthusiasm in your life?

Don, an outplacement counselor who owns his own firm, replies, "First, I always sell the person on him- or herself."

The premise, he points out, is simple; to build the out-of-work employee's confidence by focusing on the things he or she felt proud of in the past, before working on a resume outline or interview techniques. "I ask employees about the experiences and achievements they feel were most important in their lives, such as were they a class valedictorian or did they complete some sort of special work? Often, they will say, 'But I don't want to put *that* in my resume, do I?' because they think it won't look like anything important to a future employer. I always write it down, though, because everything that builds their confidence is important, and often it does lead to something that will give them an advantage during the interview or the selection process."

Don also has some advice for projecting confidence when applying with a prospective employer: Show the company what *you* have to offer *them*. "There are a lot of different ways to approach the job-search process, a lot of different ways to write a resume, and then you have to read up on each company—annual reports, company publications, and talk with people who work there. It's a tough road to travel. People are bombarded with what they should do on the outside, but the most important factor is on the inside, in attitude. You need to get pumped up about yourself and show what *you* can bring to the job."

Mastering Motivation

"When I lost my job, I was so depressed that I laid around my apartment for two weeks eating junk food and watching soap operas," says Sondra, a former travel agency manager. "Then I thought, 'This is stupid; I'm wrecking myself over a job! I'm better than this, and anyone who used to work with me who could see me now would think that I deserved to go.' So I got off the couch and cleaned up my act pretty quickly after that. Now," she smiles, "I have my own agency."

Jeff, an engineering consultant, remembers, "I saw the ax coming, but I didn't expect it to be me that had to leave. I was so angry that I got up Monday morning and challenged myself to see how quickly I could get hired—and prove that I was more valuable than my last company considered me to be."

Says Donna, a former executive secretary, "My husband was great; he wouldn't let me sit around at home just because I didn't have a job. He didn't give me time to sulk. He sat down with me and we made up a list of everything we had to take care of for our family, then we told the kids, and we all made a big checklist of things I could do and people I could talk to to get a new job. It brought us all closer together."

"It took me about a week to get going," remarks Kevin, a teacher for a small college. "I wandered around a lot, just thinking about everything except what I needed to be doing. Then one night I just sat down and convinced myself I had the determination to start looking for work."

11

Six Weeks and Counting:
Keeping Your Chin Up and Your Costs Down

Suddenly, you realize time has flown by. It usually happens after six or eight weeks, after you have been sending resumes, calling contacts, interviewing with prospective employers, and generally getting your act back together in your spare time. You look back and think, Wow! Did I really lose my job *that* long ago? And have I really applied and interviewed at *that* many places since then?

About this time, the secondary blues set in. OK, you think, I know my skills. I'm smart. I'm ambitious. I'm a good worker who can offer a lot to a good company. But out of all the people that I've talked to and all the forms I've filled out and all the businesses I've visited—Why hasn't someone hired me?!

There are plenty of reasons, most of them over which you have no control. Like the cutback process, the hiring of employees also depends on many factors:

- The national, state, and local economies

- The expansion and profit of your field

- The company's profit status; i.e., need for and ability to afford hiring new workers

- The number of available employees in your field and at your level

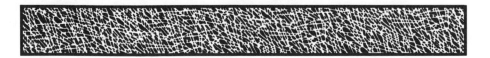

- Timing (Is there a need for engineers right now? Will the job market get better for teachers in the next five years? and so forth)

There are some factors, though, which you can control during your job search. Are they the key to what is holding you back? Double-check the following qualities in your hunt for a new position:

- **Your flexibility.** Are you only looking for one specific job, in one specific field? Or are you flexible enough to apply for positions on several different levels in several different career areas?

- **Your image.** Is it the same in every interview, or do you change it depending on the industry, company, and position for which you're applying? For example, is your outfit more conservative for a large accounting firm and a bit more creative for a college or design-firm position? Your image says a lot about your personality, and if you look like you'll fit in, you're one step closer to getting a job.

- **Your cover letter and resume.** Are you adjusting it to the person and position for which you're applying? Personalizing the name and title, and specifying the job position gives the employer a clue that you look at details, and get them right. Score another point!

- **Your horizons.** Are you searching only in your area, or are you willing to expand your possibilities throughout the county, the state, even the country or on an international scope?

- **Your attitude.** Do you appear determined, professional, enthusiastic, and honest? Nothing kills an interview like anger, depression, or guilt; leave those old emotions at home!

EMERGENCY EXITS

A job isn't going to fall in your lap right away, but after a few weeks, if your prospects still aren't looking up and you're becoming discouraged, don't lose hope. There are many more ways to creatively expand your job search, as well as earn some extra money to help you make ends meet. For example, in your job search, have you thought about:

1. **The local employment bureau:** As mentioned in chapter 8, your unemployment office should have some type of career center that can offer job leads not listed in the paper, and it's available only to those who are unemployed, not those who are looking to switch jobs. Use their sources!

2. **Trade publications:** No matter what your field, your local main library should carry all sorts of trade magazines and journals for and about workers and managers in the industry, and they usually have Help Wanted ads in the back. If your library doesn't carry them, ask the president or executive director of organizations in the fields you're tar-

geting; they'll usually be happy to loan you some of the publications they receive. Don't ignore these valuable resources!

3. **Out-of-town papers:** Your library should also carry newspapers from around the country and the world. These are especially useful for mobile workers who don't have to worry about pulling a spouse out of a job, selling a house, or changing their childrens' schools. Pick up the Sunday Help Wanted sections of newspapers from other cities with which you are familiar and where you might want to work. Hint: To get your resume across the country in time to meet an application deadline, you may have to use Federal Express or another type of one-day mailing service.

4. **Career counselors and job-placement services:** For a fee, career counselors and job-placement offices will help you re-enter the job market with services ranging from help with resumes and taped interviews to a file of job openings and recommendation services. A word of warning, however: Check out the services and the fees before you sign up, and talk to other employees who have used the company previously to make sure you'll get your money's worth of opportunities.

5. **Part-time work:** If you really need immediate money to pay bills, why not give part-time work a try? Or, sign up with a temporary agency. The work is varied, the pay can be decent, and you'll have the flexibility to still interview and job hunt during the day.

You also can take a night job if it doesn't interrupt your schedule. Night jobs usually pay ten percent or more than the average day's wage. You can try for seasonal employment as well; UPS or retail stores during the holidays, restaurants and tourist attractions during the summer season. Don't be embarrassed about it. If you need extra money, you need extra money, and these days nearly everyone is doing all they can to earn extra funds. Besides, and most importantly, you're doing something to better your situation.

6. **Seminars and job fairs:** A good place to find prospective employers, network, hand out resumes, and take on-the-spot interviews is at a local employment seminar or job fair. These are employers looking for good people to work for them, so check your local convention and visitors bureau for a listing of dates near your area.

STAYING MOTIVATED

This is the toughest part, especially when you know just how much you have to offer employers and no one seems to listen or care. Even your family and your friends are on your back about your job search—as if you weren't trying! The last thing you want to do is lose your motivation, however, so keep your chin up and your energy going, even through the worst days. Here's how:

• **Go easy on yourself.** You're working hard and you know it, even if no one else seems to understand. Every once in a while, give yourself a reward. Read a great book, rent a classic movie, make pizza—do something you love, and feel good about it.

• **Take a break.** If you get away right after you lose your job, you probably won't enjoy your time off because you'll dread going back, and you'll postpone doing the things you need to do to secure another career, ultimately stalling your road to recovery. But, after several weeks, when you have things going and under control, you may well need a break. And this time, you not only deserve it, but you'll enjoy it more, knowing that a lot of companies have your letters in their hands and your image in their minds. You're not delaying reality, either, but simply taking a hard-earned break from it to sit back and recharge your energy.

• **Laugh.** Yeah, being out of work stinks, but life in general isn't fair. You, however, are going to make the best of it, get through it, and be able to help others after you've achieved success. So don't let every little failure get you down, and take a little of the time you've been given to enjoy the small things that make life so interesting.

Take pleasure in the fact that you can:

–Spend more time with your family and friends

–See the sun and get outside in the fresh air instead of being cooped up in a cramped, windowless office with dusty air that's always too hot or too cool

–Appreciate the discipline of those who work at home, including you!

–Go to your appointments without worrying about how long they're taking or that you have to rush back to make it within your lunch hour

–Be flexible in your schedule

–Have time to exercise and take care of yourself

–Have time to think, to wonder, and to learn

–Have the chance to make choices

• **Stop what-if-ing!** If you're using the phrase when examining possibilities, fine, but if you're thinking "what if I would have done this or that," drop the thought. You can't change the past, so learn from it, but focus on the future.

• **Look back at your list of goals and skills.** Then add on to it as you go. Reminding yourself of your proven capabilities is a surefire way to keep your motivation high because you have the intelligence and drive to use them to their highest levels.

• **Spend time with people who encourage you.** It could be a friend, a parent, a spouse, or a sibling, but whomever it is, you need his or her encouragement, so don't neglect your relationships during your job search. If these people needed a positive push, you'd give it to them, so don't hesitate to ask for their inspiration.

- **Develop new skills.** Learning a new skill or trade shows prospective employers that you are flexible and willing to put your energy to work to expand your possibilities. Computer classes, writing courses, and speaking seminars are just a few ways to add to your job skills that will pay off in the future because of their broad applications. And, you can place those credentials on your resume or bring them up in interviews to show your commitment to growth and learning. Look in your local phone book or in your library directories for organizations that offer free or low-cost classes. Colleges are another resource to check into as well.

- **Enter contests.** For very little money, you can show off your skills by entering industry competitions: writing reports, art, design, exams for knowledge, and so on. Not only will you get the chance to talk with others from your field, but you will often receive advice from judges and experts if you ask. And, if you come away with any awards, it's more proof of your talent and capabilities.

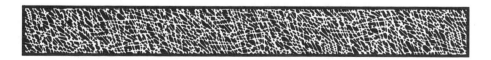

12

Glancing Backwards: A Look At What You've Learned

Six months ago, did you ever imagine you would be where you are today? Did you ever think you could learn so much, or accomplish so much? Did you ever believe you could get through it?

Of course you did, if only somewhere in the smallest shadow of your mind. Now you have, and there are a lot of people who look up to you and admire you for your skills, your strength, your courage, and your ability to turn what could have been a bad break into something that changed your life in a positive way.

And, in the course of your experience, you not only learned a lot about yourself, but you picked up many new skills and strengths as well. What are some of the things you discovered? Use chart 12.1 to list the things you have learned from your job loss and the trip forward to a better life, both mentally and physically. Write underneath each space when you realized you had that particular strength or skill.

Now, think about what your greatest accomplishments were throughout the process of realizing your job was in jeopardy, losing it, and picking yourself up from the blow to find another, and more satisfying career. Did it spur you to ask for more during the job interview process? Did you take a chance and branch out on your own? Did it bring your family closer together, affirm your independence, or give you the confidence you needed to search for a position that better fit your needs?

CHART 12.1

Looking Back on Lessons Learned

What did the loss of your job and the process of finding a new position, exploring your options, and choosing your future teach you?

New skills or strengths you learned:

What made you realize you had this skill or strength? When did you realize that it was a part of your character?

1. _____   _____

   _____

2. _____   _____

   _____

3. _____   _____

   _____

4. _____   _____

   _____

5. _____   _____

   _____

6. _____   _____

   _____

7. _____   _____

   _____

8. _____   _____

   _____

continued

9. _____　　_____

_____

10. _____　　_____

_____

On chart 12.2, write down your best accomplishments during this time, and list a brief description of the reasons why.

As the saying goes, every cloud has a silver lining, and you had the courage and the initiative to use your talent and brains to avoid the storm that could have completely wiped you out of the job market and swept away all your hope with its force. The key to your success was—and always will be—your motivation, and the key to that is your attitude, your belief in yourself to take charge of your life from the moment you realized you could.

Good luck! But then again, you don't need it. Because your future is yours to choose.

CHART 12.2

Show What You Have Accomplished

What are some of the most important things you learned through this process?

Why do you feel proud of learning them?

1. _____

_____

_____

2. _____

_____

_____

3. _____

_____

_____

4. _____

_____

_____

5. _____

_____

_____

6. _____

_____

_____

7. _____

_____

_____

8. _____

_____

_____

9. _____

_____

_____

10. _____

_____

CASE 19
Staying on the New Job Trail

"When the plant where I worked closed, I thought I would have no trouble finding a new job," admits Robert, a researcher with a degree in biology. "But I didn't take into account the economy or the number of people who blew me away with their experience. Now it takes a Ph.D. to get hired, not just a four-year or master's degree."

Robert says that after nearly three months of looking full-time for a new job, he decided to take a step back and explore other avenues for his skills and experience. "I found that I was focusing my job search much too narrowly," he says. "I was just looking for the same position or one a step above it, in the same type of company. I realized that there were a lot of other companies, smaller and larger, and not just on my side of the country, who could use my qualifications."

Susan, an executive in communications, also found herself burned out in her job hunt several weeks after she had been fired. "I felt like I was going in circles, sending out the same cover letter and saying the same things in all my interviews. So I took a break for a week and went out of town, leaving my answering machine on to catch any prospects."

She says that when she returned, her energy was recharged, her attitude had turned around, and she had regained the enthusiasm and hope that she needed to continue. "I think I had started to sound discouraged to any employer I spoke with," she adds, "because none of them really responded to my interest in their positions. But when I returned, I had three interviews set up, and two of them made me an offer!"

CASE 20
A Few Lessons Learned

"What did losing my job teach me?" muses Natalie, an architect with a small firm. "I guess I learned to really rely on myself. I never had any kind of confidence about my abilities, but after I was laid off, I realized that *I* was responsible for proving my worth to other companies. No one was going to do it for me, and if I really wanted to continue my career, I had to show them that I believed in what I could do."

"I learned to schedule my time and make lists," says Jim, who now is a supervisor in a production plant. "If I didn't have anything written down on a piece of paper, I wouldn't do it, no matter how important it was. When I started writing things down, I'd go through and organize them, and then I could check them off as I did them. It was like following a battle plan, and it taught me just how valuable time can be when there's no money coming into your account."

"I have a lot more talents than I thought I did," points out Scott, an engineer. "I always thought of myself as the shy, quiet type who could only deal with numbers, but when I lost my job I asked around about doing seminars with different organizations. Who knew I could put together classes, write plans, and stand up in front of a crowd where people would actually listen? Not me!" he grins. "I turned out to be a real ham."

"I never knew I had a backbone," admits Marlene, a shy business executive. "Losing my job made me just angry enough to start asking for what I wanted, because I realized how much I was missing by not making it clear to the people I worked with what I needed to have done. At the job I have now, I actually negotiated for a better salary than they offered. I got several thousand dollars more than I thought I would. I know a lot of people, especially men, take that for granted, but it's something I would never have had the courage to do before."

"The thing I came away from the experience with that was most valuable to me was the knowledge that I had to be more flexible about life, and that nothing is certain," advises Nick, a personnel counselor who took time out to continue his education before going back to the working world. "I used to have this great plan for my life . . . that I would take certain steps to reach a specific goal. I took it for granted that everything would go my way; it always did before. But after I lost my job, it dawned on me that there were a lot of alternatives out there that I had been refusing to look at, and some of them were better than the goals I had been planning. So I took some time to think about them and to re-evaluate what I was doing with my life. I still have the same drive to succeed, but I'm a lot more flexible about how I do it. And now I slow down to look at the opportunities that are thrown my way."